Oxford Heritage Wal

Oxford Heritage Walks
from Oxford Castle to St Giles'

Malcolm Graham

Illustrated by Edith Gollnast   *Edith Gollnast* .

OXFORD
PRESERVATION
TRUST

www.oxfordpreservation.org.uk

Oxford Preservation Trust

www.oxfordpreservation.org.uk

First published in the Great Britain 2013

Illustrations produced by Edith Gollnast
Map produced by Alun Jones

A catalogue of this book is available from the British Library
ISBN 978-0-95767-970-2

Printed and bound at Berforts Information Press Limited

Contents

About Oxford Preservation Trust   page 6

Table of Illustrations   page 7

Foreword   page 9

WALKS

1 Oxford Castle to St Michael's Street   page 13

2 Cornmarket Street to Gloucester Street   **page** 29

3 Friars Entry to St Giles'   page 39

4 Little Clarendon Street to Beaumont Street   page 59

5 Gloucester Green to Bulwarks Lane   page 69

You can follow all five parts to complete the circuit or enjoy two shorter circular walks by combining parts 1, 2 and 5 or parts 3 and 4.

About Oxford Preservation Trust

Oxford Preservation Trust is a well-established and forward-thinking charity who own, restore and care for land and buildings in the city, its setting and its views. We work hard to conserve and enhance Oxford, to give the public access to it, and to share and encourage an interest in its history. The Trust recognises that Oxford will change and develop over time and seeks to guide and not to stop, this change to Oxford's heritage.

"Oxford is growing. Its growth may be guided but should not be grudged. The work of the Trust is not to hamper Oxford but to help it. The beauty of Oxford is one of the treasures of the world."

Sir Michael Sadler, founder Trustee, OPT Annual Report (1927)

This guide records some of these changes to our beautiful city, filling in the gaps – lost buildings and memories - so that we can make sense of Oxford's rich history, appreciate and enjoy it now and in the future. It offers a reminder of the contribution more modest buildings and features make to our enjoyment of the streetscapes and skyline and their importance to the city as a whole. We are delighted that these Heritage Walks will enable a new audience to get to know and appreciate more about Oxford.

Debbie Dance, Director, 2013

Oxford Preservation Trust would like to thank the Greening Lamborn Trust, CPRE Oxfordshire Buildings Preservation Trust, the Barnsbury Charitable Trust and the William Delafield Charitable Trust for their generous donations to this project. and Alun Jones for his wonderful map.

The Greening Lamborn Trust's objective is to promote public interest in the history, architecture, old photographs and heraldry of Oxford and its neighbourhood by supporting publications and other media that create access to them.

Table of Illustrations

Frontispiece – Illustration montage On Foot in Oxford no. 9: North-West of Carfax (1980)

1 Oxford Castle to St Michael's Street

1. Oxford Castle and St George's Tower
2. Norman capitals from St George's Church crypt
3. Oxford Castle mound and Nuffield College tower
4. St. Peter's College from New Road
5. Old County Hall
6. Former Probate Registry, New Road
7. Tirah Memorial, Bonn Square
8. New Road Baptist Church
9. Book sculpture, Bonn Square
10. Methodist Meeting House and 24 & 22 New Inn Hall Street
11. Parish boundary stone, 40 New Inn Hall Street
12. City wall bastion off New Inn Hall Street
13. Former Maltby's bookbindery, St Michael's Street
14. Northgate Hall, St Michael's Street
15. St. George & Dragon sculpture, St Michael's Street
16. Dragon finial, 37 Cornmarket Street

2 Cornmarket Street to Gloucester Street

17. 28 Cornmarket Street
18. North Gate and St. Michael's Church after John Malchair print, 1788
19. Martyrs' cell door in tower of St Michael's Church
20. St. George's Mansions, Cornmarket Street
21. Carvings, William Baker House, at Broad Street corner
22. St. Mary Magdalen Church, ironwork and tomb
23. Debenhams frontage, Magdalen Street
24. Painted plaster Art Deco panel, New Theatre auditorium
25. Red Lion public house

3 Friars Entry to St Giles'

26. Friars Entry

27. Randolph Hotel canopy, Beaumont Street

28. Detail of the Martyrs' Memorial, Magdalen Street

29. Ironwork to women's underground toilets, Magdalen Street

30. Former cabmen's shelter, St Giles'

31. Statues on Taylor Institution facing St Giles'

32. Beaumont Street looking towards Worcester College in the 1820s

33. St John's College gate tower, St Giles'

34. Stone carvings, 66-67 St Giles'

35. Pusey House Chapel, St Giles'

36. Console head at Oxfam Bookshop, 56 St Giles'

37. Arms of Regent's Park College, St Giles'

38. St Giles' Café

39. Iron balconies and railings, 45-46 St Giles'

40. Northgate Hundred stone, front garden of 42 St Giles'

41. The Barn at St John's College, St Giles'

42. Arms of Samuel Wilberforce, 39a St Giles'

43. St Giles's Fair

4 Little Clarendon Street to Beaumont Street

44. Duke of Cambridge, 5 Little Clarendon Street

45. Rewley House, Wellington Square

46. Cartouche tablet of the Duke of Wellington, 3 Wellington Square

47. Cast-iron mud scrapers, St John Street

48. Former British Council offices, Beaumont Place

49. Medieval window stone tracery, back wall of 28 Beaumont Street

50. Ironwork balconies, Beaumont Street

51. Rubble stone house, Worcester Street

5 Gloucester Green to Bulwarks Lane

52. Stone sculpted panel, Old School, Gloucester Green

53. Former Settling Room, Gloucester Green, demolished 1987

54. Bas relief plaque, Odeon Cinema, George Street

55. Former City of Oxford High School for Boys, George Street

56. Victorian Pillar Box, George Street

57. Sculpted fireman's helmet, Old Fire Station, George Street

58. Former Co-op store, George Street

59. Coade stone cartouche of Britannia, Canal House, Bulwarks Lane

Foreword

This book is the first in a proposed series of Oxford Heritage Walks which will revisit and expand upon the On Foot in Oxford leaflets and booklets published by Oxford City Libraries and Oxfordshire County Libraries between 1973 and 1988. Twelve of these trails were published in all, two of them being subsequently revised and reissued under variant titles. They were written by Malcolm Graham, Local Studies Librarian for Oxford City until 1974 and for Oxfordshire from 1974. Local artists supplied the drawings, Laura Potter illustrating the first eight trails and Edith Gollnast the others. Edith also provided additional drawings for the two revised booklets. Oxford Preservation Trust gratefully acknowledges copyright permission from Oxfordshire County Council to reuse text and illustrations from these publications.

Like the earlier trails, the Oxford Heritage Walks seek to encourage interest in the history of the City and the evolution of the built environment. They are not primarily guides to Oxford's world-famous architectural treasures for which there are many alternative sources. Rather, they will explore how each area has developed and focus attention especially on streets and buildings of local importance which add character to every corner of our City. They are envisaged as a treasure-chest of information about Oxford and as a veritable arsenal of historical evidence for defending those features which make the City a special place. In support of that role, the text of each walk with full bibliographical references will also be available online at www. oxfordpreservation.org.uk

Author

Malcolm Graham read History at Nottingham University before doing a postgraduate librarianship course in Leeds and an M.A. in English Local History at Leicester University. He came to Oxford in 1970 as the City's first full-time local history librarian and took on the same role for the County in 1974. Between 1991 and 2008, he was Head of Oxfordshire Studies with Oxfordshire County Council. He has published extensively on local history – his first On Foot in Oxford town trail appeared in 1973 - and he has given hundreds of talks and broadcasts over the years. He was awarded a PhD by Leicester University for a study of the development of Oxford's Victorian suburbs and he is a Fellow of the Society of Antiquaries of London. Away from local history, he enjoys walking, cycling, outdoor swimming, music and the theatre. He is married and lives in Botley.

Illustrator

Edith Gollnast studied art and design at Banbury School of Art and architectural conservation at Bristol University. For thirty five years she worked with historic buildings and areas at Oxford City Council. Edith lives in Oxford, where amongst other pursuits she does freelance illustration

The numbers on the map refer to the illustration number

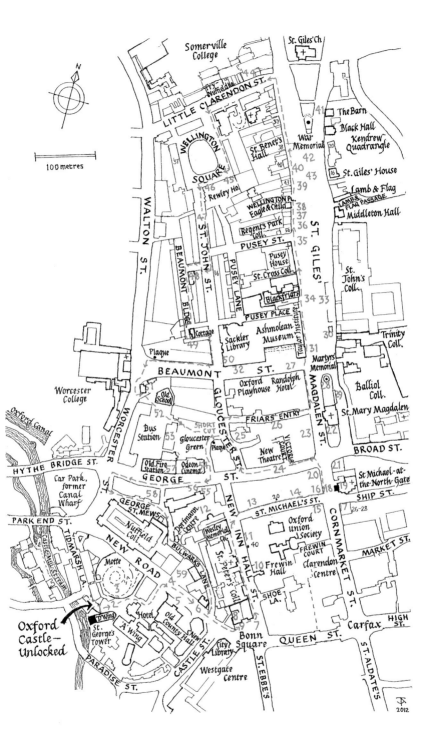

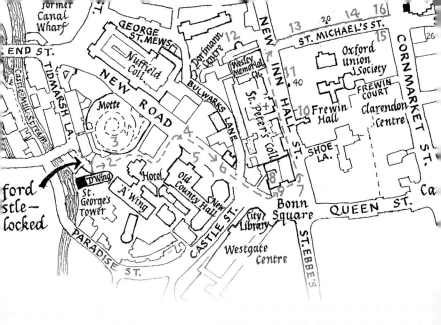

1 Oxford Castle to St Michael's Street

The walk begins within Oxford Castle, at the entrance to Oxford Castle Unlocked, where you can visit historic sites and buildings that were largely hidden from view until Oxford Prison closed in 1996. Oxford Preservation Trust created this heritage interpretation centre (2004–6, Panter Hudspeth and Richard Griffiths) as part of the successful restoration and redevelopment of Oxford Castle by Trevor Osborne Property Group and Oxfordshire County Council. Standing here, you can travel back through a thousand years of history and there is a time-line on the ground to help you. The motte or mound behind you was part of the motte and bailey castle built by Robert d'Oilly in 1071 just five years after the Norman Conquest. A ten-sided

stone keep replaced a wooden one by the 13th century and, although the ruined tower was demolished in 1650, its foundations still lie beneath the grass on the top of the mound. A visit to the mound offers excellent views over Oxford – imagine how much more you would have seen from the tall keep – and you can also go down into the castle's 13th century vaulted well chamber.

St George's Tower, massively built of rubble stone, is a remarkable defensive structure, rising in four slightly receding stages with a later diagonally set staircase in one corner. It is traditionally dated to the founding or re-founding of the church of St George's in the Castle in 1074, but it sits uncomfortably close to the mound and is now thought to have been built in

1. Oxford Castle and St George's Tower

c.1020 as a watchtower strengthening the town's western defences. The tower of St. Michael at the Northgate Church, which we shall see later in the walk, had the same role in the northern defences.

Oxford Castle is best known for King Stephen's three month siege of the Empress Matilda in 1142, which ended when she escaped over the wall during a snowstorm, dressed in white, and made her way to Wallingford. The castle was held for King John by Fawkes de Breauté in 1216 when it was besieged by baronial forces. Shire courts and assizes were held within the castle at Shire Hall until the Black Assize of 1577, when gaol fever broke out during the trial of Rowland Jenks, 'a saucy foul-mouthed bookseller'. Over 300 people, including the Lord Chief Baron and the High Sheriff, are said to have died and subsequent courts were held in the Town Hall until 1843. The

castle was used as a gaol as early as the 12th century and, although it was allowed to decay from the mid 14th century, the prison was retained. During the Civil War, the Castle was garrisoned by the Royalists. Parliamentary prisoners were housed there in unhealthy conditions, which were blamed on Smith, the gaoler. In 1649, the Commonwealth army temporarily re-fortified the castle, only to destroy the new work two years later. The gaol continued to be housed in a building next to St. George's Tower where John Wesley, founder of the Methodist movement, visited and ministered to the prisoners in 1738. The prison reformer John Howard, criticized the small, overcrowded and verminous prison in 1777 and the county magistrates built a new County Gaol between 1785 and 1805 under the supervision of William Blackburn, the pioneering prison designer. High perimeter walls were built to prevent prisoners from escaping. You will notice that part of the late 18th century prison wall has been levelled at this point now that access, rather than security, is the priority. The two storey stone range in front of you (*c.*1795–1805, William Blackburn & Daniel Harris) was the debtors' wing, built after the completion of the felons' and convicts' wing. This range, later known as D Wing, originally had a vaulted ground floor which was partially open to the outside to improve air circulation; an external balcony gave access to part of the first floor on this side of the building. The circular debtors' tower, furthest from St George's Tower, retains its original cell doors and partitions. Prisoners erected all these buildings under the watchful eye of their gaoler, Daniel Harris (*c.*1760–1840), who was also a builder, civil engineer and

architect. He had strong archaeological interests and ensured that the Norman capitals from the crypt of St George's Church were rebuilt in an atmospheric crypt beneath D Wing.

Walk towards New Road, noticing the juxtaposition of the castle mound and Nuffield College tower and spire built in the 1950s. Turn right beyond cycle racks, passing between the stone-built former Governor's House (1847–8, Benjamin Ferrey) and a modern building (2004–6, Sir Jeremy Dixon), which provides restaurant and hotel accommodation with a roof garden on the site of 20th century prison warders' houses. Emerging into the paved avenue beside Old County Hall, you have a fine view, away to your right, of the castellated prison frontage, now the entrance to

2. Norman Capitals from St George's Church crypt

3. Oxford Castle mound and Nuffield College tower

the Oxford Malmaison Hotel. By the 1840s, the gaol had become too small and A Wing (1852–6, H. J. Underwood & J. C. Buckler) behind this frontage provided additional cells on three levels. The design followed the 'separate' system pioneered at Pentonville, where prisoners in solitary confinement could reflect on the consequences of their crimes. The closure of Oxford Prison, first suggested in 1946, led to the brilliant, if improbable, conversion of these premises into luxury hotel accommodation (2004–6, Architects Design Partnership with Jestico & White).

Turn left up the avenue leading to New Road, noting on your right the castellated flanking wing wall to Old County Hall, which terminates in a tiny turret. The blocked doorway in the wall originally gave access to a men's urinal. New Road was new in 1769–70, built by the Botley and Newland Turnpike Trust between Castle Street and Hollybush Row to link

up with an improved Botley Road and the newly-built Swinford Bridge. The Norman castle had overlaid part of Saxon Oxford, obstructing the western exit from the city, and New Road cut through the castle bailey on its way to Fisher Row. Christ Church owned much of the castle site at that time and ensured that the mound was retained 'as an ornament to that District, and as a venerable Monument of Antiquity.' The college successfully defended the mound again in 1848 when railway contractors wanted to plunder it for building materials.

The portion of the castle bailey north of New Road became the Coal Wharf of the Oxford Canal, which reached Oxford on January 1st, 1790. The canal brought cheaper coal to the city and the arrival of the first boats was accompanied by church bells and bands. The wharf closed in 1937 and Nuffield College now occupies most of the site. Two gargantuan stone gate pillars opposite marked the entrance to the wharf but now lead to St Peter's College car park. Beyond the car park, you can see the portico and side elevation of Canal House (1827–9, Richard Tawney), which is now the Master's Lodgings for St Peter's College.

Turn right up New Road, noting the fine pavement, which was a by-product of the Castle development. Sir Charles Oman dismissed Old County Hall (1840–1, John Plowman) as 'quite the most abominable pseudo-Gothic assize court in all England, composed of mock-Norman arches, pepper box turrets, meaningless machicolation, arrow-slits in inaccessible places, and large round topped windows'. The building is now listed as a 'delightful Neo-Norman fortress with Georgian-type windows in Gothic surrounds' and it is frequently photographed. Notice beside the gateways and the main door, stone piers topped by cast iron fasces and modern, traditionally designed lanterns. Fasces, bundles of wooden sticks with an axe blade emerging from the centre, were symbols of the Roman republic and they are widely used as symbols of power and jurisdiction. The eastern flanking wing wall was unfortunately removed for the building of the adjacent New County Hall (1971–4, County Architect's Office/ Albert Smith), a glass and concrete office block which is very much of its time. A mature copper beech tree masks the link block between the old and new buildings. Notice the traditional Oxfordshire signpost and a turnpike milestone, both re-sited beyond the tree. The 1930s signpost stood originally at a crossroads near Bloxham and the milestone of *c*.1755 was on the Oxford to Banbury road.

4. St. Peter's College from New Road

5. Old County Hall

Across the road, notice no. 10A New
Road, the former Probate Registry (1863,
Charles Buckeridge), an attractive stone
building in late 13th century style, which
is unsymmetrical with its gables and
tall chimneys. Beyond the entrance to
Bulwarks Lane – which we shall explore
later in the walk – stands the red brick
building occupied by The Bell & Compass
and the Co-operative Bank. It is on the
site of the Anchor pub which, with its
extensive yard and stables, was once an
important stopping point for country
carriers. The next building (c.1860), on
the corner of Bonn Square, is almost
triangular in shape, and makes use of an
odd site left over when New Road was
cut through Castle Street.

On the opposite side of the road,
the Westgate Centre (1969–73, City
Architect's Office/Douglas Murray) is of
complex plan. Linking with Pennyfarthing
Place to the East, Castle Street to the

West and a multi-storey car park to the South, the Centre was intended to 'form a natural extension to the existing shopping [area], providing a much-needed increase in the number of shops in the centre of the City'. Pedestrians are protected from the weather by a glazed roof and from traffic by a basement level service road. Above the shops to the right of the main arcade, a new Central Library was provided and opened on May 17th, 1973. The Westgate Centre was refurbished in 1986 and the 'bandstand' outside the main arcade was part of that improvement. Ambitious but controversial plans to revamp the existing Centre and extend it South to Thames Street secured planning permission in 2007 but the scheme is on hold at present.

Bonn Square was transformed in 2008–9 after Graeme Massie Architects, a Scottish firm, won an international competition to re-design this valuable city centre space. The Tirah Memorial (1900, Inigo Thomas) remains as a focal point for the new square and recalls men of the Oxfordshire & Buckinghamshire Light Infantry who died in a campaign against tribesmen on the North-West Frontier in what is now Pakistan in 1897. The sloping paved area around the memorial is a reminder that this was the churchyard of the former St Peter le Bailey Church, raised by centuries of burials. Archaeological excavations in 2008 revealed 296 burials and 53 memorial stones on the site. St Peter le Bailey Church was first recorded in 1122 but the medieval and later building fell down in 1726. It was rebuilt in a sturdy Classical style with a west tower (*c.*1740) but this structure, which jutted out into the roadway, was demolished in 1873 as a new St Peter le Bailey Church was being completed in New Inn Hall Street. The

6. Former Probate Registry, New Road

7. Tirah Memorial, Bonn Square

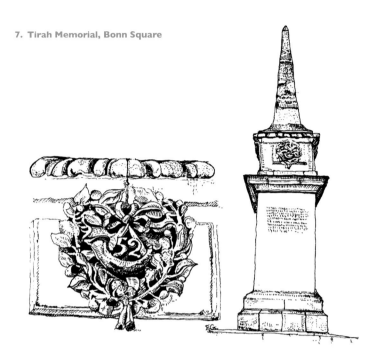

churchyard was railed off, but, in 1897, it was opened as a public garden that survived with modifications until 2008.

To the left, the re-designed Bonn Square offers a better view of New Road Baptist Church, which has an ashlar stone front with a Doric pedimented porch and two flanking niches on the first floor (1819, John Hudson; major alterations and heightening, 1865, J. F. Earle). The church developed in this discreet off-street location during the 18th century and, until 2008, its forecourt was still cut off from the street by fine Victorian railings installed in *c.* 1873. Note the stone pillar, which survives from that scheme and a Peace tablet fixed nearby to the rubble stone wall in 2010.

As you pass the Tirah Memorial, notice the two piles of books to your left and odd volumes apparently left on some of the benches. This artwork (2009, Diana Bell) was a gift from Bonn to Oxford and the piles of books cast in bronze symbolize the long-standing link between the two cities, forged in 1948. Ironically, the stone recording the official naming of Bonn Square on October 5th, 1974 was lost during the refurbishment in 2008. In its place, you will see a plaque on the side elevation of no. 1 New Inn Hall Street recalling the 1974 event and the reopening of the new Bonn Square in May 2009. No. 1 is a three storey timber framed house with a vast stone chimney stack, dating from the early 17th century, with 18th century sash windows and later shop fronts. The home of Richard Bettris

8. New Road Baptist Church

(c. 1606–1682), a surgeon and well-known Quaker, this building was Oxford's first Quaker meeting house from 1654 until the early 1680s.

Go down the steps and turn left into New Inn Hall Street, attractively re-designed as a shared space for drivers, cyclists and pedestrians in 2009. The street was known as North Bailey by 1399 and a later name, The Seven Deadly Sins, current between c. 1570 and 1800, probably derived from a pub sign or from seven poor cottages. The current name recalls New Inn Hall, an academic hall built on the site of Trilleck's Inn (c. 1460), which stood on the west side of the street. During the Civil War (1642–6), its buildings were used as Charles 1's Royal Mint and the famous Oxford Crown piece was struck there. The largely 18th century front of no. 5, the last property before the former Girls' Central School,

was retained in the redevelopment of premises next to New Road Baptist Church and incorporates part of the façade of New Inn Hall.

On the other side of the street, North Bailey House (1974–5, Collins, Stonebridge & Bradley) replaced

9. Book sculpture, Bonn Square

Newspaper House (1880). This building had been Walter Higgins' furniture warehouse and, from 1928 to 1972, the home of the *Oxford Mail* and *Times*. Down Shoe Lane, a corruption of Sewys Lane, St. Michael's Hall is a tall, four storey brick building (1875, F. J. Codd). It was part of Hyde's clothing factory, a sizeable employer of labour in Oxford before the motor industry. To the north of Shoe Lane, the Brasenose College Frewin Hall development scheme (1980, Architects Design Partnership/John Fryman) replaced the former St. Michael's School (1876, E. G. Bruton), which consisted of a master's house with schoolroom behind. Part of the historic Frewin Hall boundary wall in Shoe Lane was retained in the scheme.

Opposite Shoe Lane, St Peter's College now occupies the former Oxford Central Girls' School (1901, Leonard Stokes). The stone-faced frontage is recessed between wings and the attractive iron railings are 1980s replicas of originals lost to wartime salvage. A wall tablet, 'Pupil Teachers' Centre', on the south wing recalls efforts by Oxford School Board to regularize the training of pupil teachers, who were children of 13 plus apprenticed to head teachers in order to learn the craft of teaching by example and practice.

Next to the former school stands Hannington Hall (1832, Thomas Greenshields), also now part of St. Peter's College, which has an ashlar stone front of five bays, bays one and five being flanked by large pilasters. It was envisaged as the first stage of an ambitious scheme to revitalize New Inn Hall but no further building took place and the hall was united with Balliol College in 1882. The present name recalls James Hannington (1847–85), the martyred missionary Bishop of Eastern Equatorial Africa, and dates from alterations (1896–7, Walter Shirley) carried out for the Oxford Inter-Collegiate Christian Union and Missionary Union.

Back on the east side of New Inn Hall Street, nos. 22–24, though apparently of 17th century domestic origin with tall cocklofts, proved to be two bays of a single storey range (c.1500–30), fronting St. Mary's College, a small college of Augustinian canons founded in 1436. Oak lintels above the doorways record earlier house numbers, 13 and 14, in Roman numerals. Nos. 26–30 form a pleasant courtyard group (c.1870) enclosed by the chestnut trees of the garden beyond. Further along the street, Oxford's first Methodist Meeting House (c.1780) bears a plaque recording that John Wesley preached here on July 14th, 1783, and on subsequent occasions.

Next door, the 16th century gateway of St. Mary's College contains within it the springings of the vaulting of an earlier gate hall. Frewin Hall (private) is partially visible beyond, and consists, basically, of an L-shaped block. The hidden west wing was built (c.1582) for Griffith Lloyd (d.1586), Principal of Jesus College, over

10. Methodist Meeting House and 24 & 22 New Inn Hall Street

the 12th century cellar of a merchant's house, which later formed part of St. Mary's College. A second storey was added (1888, T. G. Jackson) for Dr. C. L. Shadwell, Provost of Oriel (d.1919). The south wing, a two storeyed rubble-stone building, was built in 1721 for Dr. Richard Frewin (d.1761), Camden Professor of History and a distinguished physician, whose name the house retains. A later occupant was the Prince of Wales, later Edward VII, when he was at Christ Church (1860–1). Behind the house, the steep slate roof of the Oxford Union debating hall, now the Old Library (1857,

Benjamin Woodward) is a prominent feature.

Between Frewin Hall and St. Michael's Street, the east side of New Inn Hall Street is dominated by tall, four storey brick houses from the 1860s and 1870s, which have been internally reconstructed with projecting rear stairs to the new Quad (1977, Architects Design Partnership/John Fryman). No. 38 is of polychrome bricks with carved stone capitals and no. 40 retains, at ground floor level, a parish boundary stone of 1933. On no. 50, a plaque recalls that

11. Parish boundary stone, 40 New Inn Hall Street

the Rev. Thomas Chamberlain, vicar of St. Thomas's, founded St. Edward's School on the site in 1863. The school moved to new and larger premises at Summertown in 1873. Recalling the old building, Warden Simeon remarked that, 'As a harbour for rats it was probably unique'.

Across the street again, St. Peter's College (founded as St. Peter's Hall, 1928) has taken over two important buildings. The Victorian Gothic St. Peter le Bailey Church (1874, Basil Champneys), built of Bath stone and re-used stone from the old church, has become the College chapel. Next door, Wyaston House or Linton House (1797) now forms a library and entrance to St. Peter's College. It is a fine Georgian house three storeys high with lower, one bay wings at either side. It was built for the Oxford Canal Company and became St. Peter le Bailey rectory in 1878. The name Linton House recalls Henry Linton, rector between 1856 and 1884. Modern railings featuring the keys of St. Peter as a design motif adorn the garden wall in front of the property. Further north, the Wesleyan Memorial Methodist Church (1878, Charles Bell) abandoned the Grecian style of the earlier chapel behind it (1817, W. Jenkins; demol. 1966) for soaring Gothic. The tapering steeple is beautifully situated at the north-east corner of the building, closing the view down St. Michael's Street.

12. City wall bastion off New Inn Hall Street

New Inn Hall Street was extended through the old city wall to George Street in 1872, the descent from inside the wall across the site of the ditch being quite marked. A bastion of the wall is visible in the garden behind the former High School for Boys. The extension was temporarily called Sadler Street in honour of Ald. Charles Sadler (d.1872) who, for many years, had been a power in the Liberal Corporation, but this name was soon dropped because of confusion with another Sadler Street in St. Ebbe's. New Inn Hall Street thus became T-shaped until 1899, when the part leading to Cornmarket Street was re-named St. Michael's Street. Two notable buildings in the extension of New Inn Hall Street, both now demolished, were the engine house of the Oxford Volunteer Fire Brigade (1873–4, G. Shirley), and the Liberal Hall (1877–8, F. J. Codd) where Alliance House now stands.

Turn right into St. Michael's Street, which runs parallel to and just inside the city wall. Notice on the north side, nos. 34–36, which were apparently built as one house in the late 18th century. Above the ground floor, they are timber framed, the rendering over the lath and plaster being ruled to give the appearance of stone; the sash windows flush to the wall on the first and second floors give the secret away. No. 34 was the home of Felicia Skene (1821–99) from 1869 and a blue plaque recalls her work as a friend of the poor and prison visitor. Almost opposite, nos. 17–19 and no. 11 are of similar date and character. Nos. 28–32 are small 19th century shops, with workshops above, incorporating one of the city wall bastions. Now excellently converted into Bike Zone, they were occupied until 2008 by Messrs. Alfred Maltby, Oxford bookbinders since 1834. No. 26 (c.1800) is a little brick house three storeys high

13. Former Maltby's bookbindery, St Michael's Street

14. Northgate Hall, St Michael's Street

with Flemish bond brickwork above a stuccoed ground floor. More remarkable is no. 24, which dates from the late 17th century and is of renewed ashlar stone and three storeys high with twin pedimented shaped gables back and front. No. 20, Vanbrugh House, is again 17th century but it was re-fronted early in the 1700s. It was the home of Oxford builder and master mason Bartholomew Peisley (d.1715), who presumably built it with his experience of working on Blenheim

Palace very much in mind. The building is of ashlar stone, three storeys high with giant pilasters either side of the central bay carrying 'a cornice as deep as though it were a canopy'.

Nos. 20-24 were restored and converted to form the Vanbrugh House Hotel in 2012. Northgate Hall (1870–1, J. C. Curtis) was built as a chapel and schoolroom for the United Methodist Free Church. It is of stone and classical, five bays wide, with a central pediment. Cement patches on the façade mask old commercial advertising panels. The building was transformed into a restaurant during 2013.

On the south side, a late 19th century brick wall overhung with flowering trees introduces the mainly Victorian buildings of the Oxford Union Society, which are of red brick with stone or terracotta dressings and have tiled and slated roofs. From east to west are: New Buildings (1910, W.E. Mills); the two storeyed Main Block in Venetian Gothic style (1864, its high-pitched roof (1856, Benjamin Woodward); and the Debating Hall (1878, Sir Alfred Waterhouse). East of the Union, now the Three Goats Head pub, is a three storeyed Victorian Gothic fantasy (1876), probably designed by F.J. Codd, which has heavy pillars supporting a polychrome brick facade and decorative ironwork at first floor level. Further down, the street is completed by Thomas Rayson's gabled reconstruction of the Plough public house (1925), the 14th century statue of St. George at first floor level being introduced by Rayson to fill the niche.

15. St George & Dragon sculpture, St Michael's Street

The north side ends with the stuccoed front of nos. 8–10 (c.1820) and the gables of nos. 4–6 (Arcadia and the Nosebag restaurant). These properties date back to c.1560 and originally formed part of a continuous row of timber-framed houses. On the corner,

no. 37 Cornmarket, or Northgate House (c.1860) has at first floor level a cast-iron electric lamp bracket with dragon finial (c.1895). Retained when Cornmarket was re-lighted in 1974/5, this bracket was installed when electric street lighting in Oxford was still in its infancy.

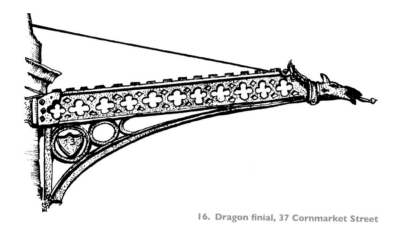

16. Dragon finial, 37 Cornmarket Street

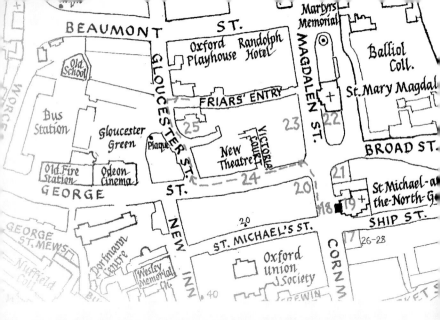

2 Cornmarket Street to Gloucester Street

ornmarket Street is now dominated by buildings erected by chain stores in a very different retail world. These include Clarendon House (1956–7, Lord Holford), built for Woolworths and occupied by the firm until 1983; also, the former Marks & Spencer building on the north corner of Market Street (1963, Lewis & Hickey); and the Littlewoods building (1964, D. M. C. Ruddick), which McDonalds now occupies. The street name 'Cornmarket' recalls its much older country and market town character, and this lingers on in just a few buildings, especially here at the northern end. Nos. 26–28, three-gabled timber-framed properties on the corner of Ship Street, are particularly interesting as one of Oxford's few surviving medieval domestic buildings. Built as the New Inn in c.1390,

the property was later subdivided and nos. 26–27 were occupied from the 1870s until 1983 by Zacharias', a firm well known for its Wet-Off waterproof clothing and the slogan 'Zacs for Macs'. Alterations to the building had left few visible traces of its antiquity but no. 28 was restored to something like its original appearance (1951, Thomas Rayson). Nos. 26–27 were later reconstructed along much more archaeological lines (1986, Architects Design Partnership/ John Fryman & F.W. B. Charles) as part of a Jesus College development. Just opposite, notice the gabled 1665 facade of no. 38, the former Plough Inn, now Austin Reed, Ltd., which was an earlier Thomas Rayson reconstruction in 1925. Next door, no. 39 (Timpson's) has a four storey 19th century front, possibly disguising an earlier core. No. 40 (Snappy

17. 28 Cornmarket Street

Snaps) is an 18th century re-fronting of a 17th century house. The canted late 18th century style bays of nos. 41–42 above the Orange store, and no. 23 (part of W H Smith's) opposite, both mask 17th century timber-framed buildings.

St. Michael at the Northgate church stands at the corner of Ship Street and Cornmarket Street, its late Saxon tower (c.1020), originating, like St. George's Tower, as a watchtower on the town's defences. It was built of Coral Rag stone with 'long and short quoins and two tiers of twin bell-openings with bulgy balusters and through stones'. A blocked west doorway, high up, originally opened on

to the adjacent North Gate. The rest of the church is of 13th–15th century date with the addition of a north transept (1833, John Plowman). Later restoration work by G. E. Street (1853–4) was largely obliterated by a serious fire in 1953.

Anthony Wood, the 17th century historian, remarked that the North Gate was the city's strongest, 'as indeed by good reason it should (be), having noe river before it as the other hath'. It was fortified with a portcullis and two gates, a military engine on the ramparts being ready to 'cast downe anything obnoxious to the enimy approaching therunto'. The town gaol was at the North Gate by

18. North Gate and St. Michael's Church after John Malchair print, 1788

1239, and became known as Bocardo, a name thought to be derived from a logician's term for a syllogism, and to imply that the prison, like a syllogism, was an awkward trap from which to escape. A more prosaic suggestion is that it derived from the word 'boccard' or 'boggard,' meaning a privy, and referred to its insanitary state. A separate room for prostitutes, later known ironically as the maidens' chamber, was provided in c.1310. Bocardo's most famous inmates were the Oxford Martyrs, Bishops Nicholas Ridley and Hugh Latimer (1555) and Archbishop Thomas Cranmer (1556), their cell door being now displayed in the tower of St. Michael's church. By 1641, Bocardo was a debtors' prison, or bridewell, and 18th

century engravings show a bag suspended from the first floor window mutely soliciting donations from passers-by. The North Gate was finally demolished in 1771 as an inconvenience to traffic, its opening being less than 11 feet wide at the narrowest point.

The northern end of Cornmarket Street was then set back and rebuilt, a fragment of this rebuilding being the bayed three light Venetian window which survives above KFC at no. 35. A building on the same site was formerly a gymnasium and dancing school attended by John Evelyn in 1638, and by the future Charles II during the Civil War. The rest of the street, above shop front level, dates from

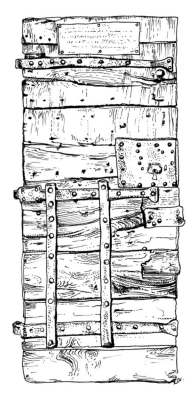

described as 'Oxford's last independent department store', officially dates back to 1738 but members of the Boswell family were in business locally as carpenters or joiners even earlier. The firm made and sold portmanteaus, trunks and cases of all sorts at nos. 49–50 Cornmarket Street until 1929 when it moved to new premises round the corner at nos. 1-3 Broad Street and rapidly evolved into a department store. The Oxford Drug Company Ltd. had, in the meantime, taken over Pearson's shop at no. 31 Cornmarket Street. Forging a link between this chemist's business and Boswell's provided further scope for expansion. These developments occupied all the land behind the pompously Classical corner building (1915, N.W. & G.W. Harrison) which was erected for William Baker & Co., and is now Waterstone's bookshop. Baker's claimed to have been established in 1795 – note the date above the shop front – but first appears as cabinet maker and upholsterer at no. 1 Broad Street in 1861. The business expanded into a three storey brick warehouse behind the shop in 1882, and that building, now much-altered, survives in Ship Street. Elliston & Cavell acquired the business in 1902 after William Baker's death, but the house furnishing store remained outwardly independent until the 1970s.

Pause before turning left into George Street, perhaps in the comparative

the late 19th or early 20th centuries. Prominent buildings on the west side are the three gabled no. 36, formerly the Northgate Tavern (1879), and St. George's Mansions (1910, Homer & Lucas), now a branch of the NatWest Bank, on the corner of George Street. The latter was described as Oxford's first skyscraper when the plans were revealed. On the east side, next to St Michael's, no. 30 is of ashlar stone and neo-Classical with a Dutch gable (1904, Herbert Quinton) and Boswell's at no. 31 has a gabled polychrome brick front (1878, F. J. Codd) originally built for Pearson's the ironmongers. Boswell's,

calm beside the leafy churchyard of
St. Mary Magdalen Church, which
has retained both iron railings and
lampholders of c.1850, and many 19th
century gravestones. Houses (demol.
c.1790) formerly occupied much of this
churchyard and another group (demol.
1820) stood to the north of the church.

The western side of Magdalen Street
was rebuilt between 1894 and 1912,
largely for the city's premier department
store, Elliston & Cavell Ltd. (founded
1823). Debenhams took over Elliston's
in 1953 and redeveloped the whole site
(1999–2000, Le Riche Maw), retaining
the impressive Victorian and Edwardian

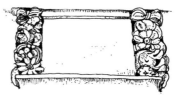

21. Carvings, William Baker House, at Broad Street corner

22. St. Mary Magdalen Church, ironwork and tomb

façades, to provide a much more space intensive store on the upper floors and separate retail units below. You therefore have here an unusual window into local retailing history, beginning on the corner of George Street with a four storey property (1895) which had a highly desirable caretaker's penthouse flat behind the corner turret. T.H. Rose, chairman of Elliston's, commissioned the building with future expansion in mind and the store eventually took it over, for menswear, in 1956. Going north, the next property (1912, G. H. Blatherwick) was Taphouse's music shop (estab. 1857; closed 1984), which also hired out concert and practice rooms

upstairs. Taphouse's had replaced the notorious Woodstock Arms pub and a correspondent remarked that 'the sweet tones of his instruments and the character of his sheet music contrast with the orgies and uncouth strains which so frequently disturbed the street and neighbourhood from the habitués of that missed house'. From 1956, Taphouse's became a barrier to shoppers at Elliston's, forcing them out into the street to get from one department to another and, when the music shop moved to Westgate in 1982, Debenhams took over the premises. Whereas Elliston's facades are vaguely Classical in style, Taphouse's old shop has a medieval look with lancet windows and grotesque carvings on the upper floors. Nos. 5–12 Magdalen Street were Elliston & Cavell's main store and, until Debenhams introduced corporate branding for all its stores in 1973, the firm's name used to be emblazoned in ornate gilded letters on the ornamental cresting above the shop fronts. Nos. 9–12 (1894, H.G.W. Drinkwater), nearest to Friars Entry, were a major Elliston's development, providing showroom space, workrooms and top floor bedrooms for shop assistants. Nos. 7-8 (1899-1900, Herbert Quinton) represented a further substantial addition to the south.

Now head into George Street past Oxford's first skyscraper! The street was known as Irishman's Street by 1251,

perhaps because 'Irishmen studied or els had commerce here' or, more probably, because of William de Hibernia, bailiff of Northgate Hundred in 1254. Early medieval settlement was abandoned after the Black Death reduced Oxford's population, and building only resumed after the City acquired the area as part of the Northgate Hundred in 1592. The Civil War interrupted development, but houses lined much of the street by 1675, and gaps were filled during the 18th century. Until *c.*1770, the street was sometimes called Thames Street, leading as it does to a branch of the river, Castle Mill Stream, at Hythe Bridge. Since then, the name George Lane, or Street, has taken over, recalling the former George

23. Debenhams frontage, Magdalen Street

Inn, established by 1395 on the corner of George Street and Magdalen Street.

It is hard to imagine that George Street once resembled today's picturesque Holywell Street. Widened and almost entirely rebuilt in the late 19th and early 20th centuries, George Street became a major commercial area and was part of the one-time 'Bunny Run,' a circuit completed by Cornmarket, Queen Street and New Inn Hall Street, where strolling groups of lads and girls could hope to meet up for a sociable evening. The Grapes public house (1894, H. G. W. Drinkwater) is a small gabled structure with an attractive red brick and terracotta frontage which was designed to complement the older, timber-framed buildings beside it. They soon made way for much larger buildings and you can see how the Grapes' chimneys had to be extended up to the roofline of nos. 9/13 George Street (1907) in order to secure the downdraught needed for the coal fires. This mighty neighbour was built as Eugene de la Mare's toyshop – notice the retained enamel advertisement for toys, fancy goods and fireworks high up on the gable end of no. 9 – but the fine brick frontage was given a rendered makeover in the 1960s.

On the other side of the street, beyond Debenhams, the letters YMCA and the date 1891 high up on nos. 6/16 George Street announce the former Young Men's Christian Association building (1891, F. W. Albury). A fire in 1966 robbed the building of some ornamentation.

On the corner of Victoria Court, no. 16 George Street is now part of Bella Italia restaurant but, in 1904, it was the head office for William Morris's Oxford Automobile and Cycle Agency. Morris Garages Ltd. used the premises as a showroom in the 1920s, displaying just one lorry in the window. Across Victoria Court, the New Theatre (1933–4, W. & F. R. Milburn) is a tall ashlar stone building with a canopy along George Street, most distinguished perhaps for its Art Deco interior. It is the fourth New Theatre in this area since 1836. The first one was in Victoria Court and was also sometimes known as the Theatre Royal or the Victoria. Social segregation of the audience was achieved by having three separate entrances, Victoria Court for standing room only, Red Lion Square for the gallery and Magdalen Street for more exclusive boxes. The theatre was often used for music hall entertainment since the University had forbidden professional drama during term-time in the late 16th century, fearing that it might corrupt or at least distract the undergraduate population. By the 1880s, the University was more welcoming and a second New Theatre (1886, H.G.W. Drinkwater), with a frontage to George Street, opened on February 13th, 1886. This theatre was rebuilt after a fire in 1892, but completely new and larger premises were necessary in 1908 (J. R. Wilkins) and again in 1933–4, as demand outgrew available space.

Continuing along George Street, nos.

24. Painted plaster Art Deco panel, New Theatre auditorium

29/31 (1924) on your left were formerly new car showrooms for City Motors (estab. 1919), which had its head office round the corner in Gloucester Street until c.1968. Next door, nos. 33/35, the former Radiant House (1926, J. R. Wilkins), were built for Hill, Upton & Co., Oxford's first electrical contractors (estab. 1890). The building has a handsome brick and stone façade with bronze panels and window frames. Originally, there were two globe lanterns on the roof, replicas of lamps designed for the contemporary British Empire Exhibition at Wembley. On the corner of New Inn Hall Street, O'Neill's Bar at no. 37 was a radical transformation of the City's former electricity showrooms in 1996.

Turn right into Gloucester Street, which was known formerly as Pudding Bag Lane. This may have been on account of its odd shape since it originally had two branches, one ending at Gloucester Green and the other in what is now Red Lion Square; perhaps, though, it was a modest tribute to the Oxford tradesmen whose culinary efforts once whetted the appetites of University men. Jamie's restaurant (opened 2008), on the corner, occupies premises which were formerly the Oxford & District Co-operative Society's gentlemen's outfitting department and you can still make out the words 'raincoats', 'sportswear', etc., in the upper panels of the windows. The neo-Georgian block opposite (1935, Wills

25. Red Lion Public House

& Kaula/J. C. Leed), which continues down George Street, replaced the George Street Congregational Chapel (1832, Thomas Greenshields) and the George Street Cinema (1911, G. W. Booth).

Beyond Jamie's, Anna Belinda were exclusive dress designers at no. 6 Gloucester Street from 1971 to 2012. Red Lion Square on your right now leads to Debenham's delivery area and the stage door of the New Theatre. Passing the Red Lion pub, which was rebuilt (1905, J. R. Wilkins) to round off a busy corner, you have a foretaste of the lively Gloucester Green redevelopment (1987-90, Kendrick Associates), which

we shall explore later. The open space opposite was occupied by the Blue Pig pub, controversially demolished to widen Gloucester Street in 1935. Described as 'one of Oxford's oldest and most picturesque taverns', the 17th century pub was frequented by 'jovial Oxfordshire farmers' on market days and by undergraduates who had a choice of exits if the proctors and their bulldogs raided the premises.

Go straight to p. 69 to shorten the walk at this point.

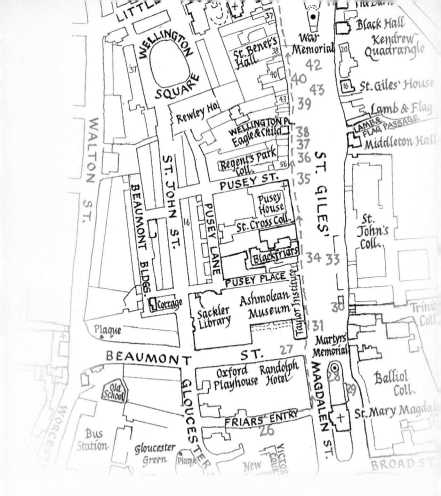

3 Friars Entry to St Giles'

Turn right beyond the Red Lion pub garden into Friars Entry, noticing the red brick Burton Taylor Studio (1973), an extension to the nearby Playhouse funded by the famous actors, Elizabeth Taylor and Richard Burton. Before Beaumont Street was laid out in 1822, Gloucester Street ended here and Friars Entry was still the most direct route from central Oxford to Worcester College. It had, in medieval times, been the way to the house of the Carmelites, or White Friars, in the former Beaumont Palace. A great gate led into medieval Friars Entry but this was probably removed after the dissolution of the religious houses in Henry VIII's reign. Crowded houses later lined the alleyway and added to the perceived remoteness of Worcester College, founded in 1714 in the surviving buildings of Gloucester College. When Dr. Landon, Provost of

26. Friars Entry

Worcester, was Vice-Chancellor (1802-6), Encaenia processions had to pass, with as much dignity as could be mustered, through Friars Entry, 'at the risk of being besprinkled by trundled mops in those straits of Thermopylae, of stumbling over buckets, knocking over children, of catching the rincings of basins, and ducking under linen-lines suspended across from the opposite houses'.

Little survives of the old Friars Entry – and, visually at least, it begins disappointingly. The car park on the left and the pub garden on the right occupy the cleared sites of good three storey brick houses built in c.1825. The alley recaptures some of its old character as it narrows at the former Gloucester Arms public house (1825), restored and re-opened as the White Rabbit in

2012 to recall Lewis Carroll's literary creation. Further along, the Debenhams development promotes a good sense of enclosure, and provided space for an appealing pub, Far From the Madding Crowd. Named after Thomas Hardy's novel, it provides a splendid retreat from Oxford's busy streets. Thomas Hardy knew Oxford well, having worked in the office of Arthur Blomfield, architect of St Barnabas' Church, between 1862 and 1867 and the city features as Christminster in his novel *Jude the Obscure*. Opposite, no. 24 Friars Entry is a three storey brick house which probably dates from the 1820s and retains a contemporary shop front with wide glazing bars. It was occupied by local estate agents, E. Gordon Hudson, for many years until 2009: the premises are now the Organic Deli café. On either side, good-looking display shop fronts formed part of a Randolph Hotel development (2002, Bell Slater Partnership) but, like Emily's shop in the classic children's television series *Bagpuss*, they don't contain anything for sale! As you continue, the 1920s side elevation of the Odeon Magdalen Street cinema becomes obvious on your left. Opposite, there are photographs of produce in shop windows but, regrettably for the liveliness of Friars Entry, no access to the Tesco Metro store.

You emerge into Magdalen Street opposite the west tower of St Mary Magdalen Church, built 1511–31, which has an image, possibly of St. Mary Magdalene, high up in a niche. Turn left past Oxenford House (1966, Fitzroy, Robinson & Partners) which replaced an earlier building that housed, among other things, Oxford's first broadcasting studio opened in 1925. Next door, the Odeon Magdalen Street, formerly the Super Cinema (1922, J. C. Leed), was an Egyptian-style development on the site of former stables taken over by Morris Garages Ltd. On the corner of Magdalen Street and Beaumont Street, the tall and Gothic Randolph Hotel (1864–5, William Wilkinson) provided Oxford with what was long described as its only modern-built hotel. Wilkinson (1819–1901) was architect to the St John's College estate in North Oxford and spent his last years in the hotel he had designed. An iron and glass canopy was built outside the main entrance in Beaumont Street in 1889 to shelter arriving or departing guests. The supporting columns bear the name 'Lucy & Co Oxford'. The Randolph was extended along Beaumont Street (1952, J. Hopgood), surprisingly in matching style at a time when Victorian Gothic was still deeply unpopular. Colin Dexter's popular fictional detective, Inspector Morse, regularly visited the hotel bar to discuss cases with his colleague Lewis and the Randolph now has a Morse Bar to perpetuate this link.

Cross Magdalen Street at the traffic lights for a closer look at St Mary Magdalen Church. The church is first recorded in *c*.1127 but its oldest surviving features are the nave and chancel, which were

27. Randolph Hotel canopy, Beaumont Street

probably rebuilt in the late 13th century. The south chapel dates from c.1320 and has replacement statues (1914, H. W. Moore) in canopied niches in its buttresses. The south porch was added in the early 16th century. The north or Martyrs' Aisle (1840–2, Scott & Moffatt) was one outcome of a nationwide appeal to build a monument to the Protestant Oxford Martyrs, Latimer, Ridley and Cranmer. In 1839, the organizing Oxford committee planned to build a church near the site of the martyrdom in Broad Street but this proved impossible. Instead, they opted for the Martyrs' Aisle and a nearby memorial inspired by the 14th century Eleanor Cross at Waltham, one of fifteen erected by Edward I to

commemorate the resting places of his Queen's body on the way to London. George Gilbert Scott & W. B. Moffatt won the design competition and the memorial was built between 1841 and 1843. Sir Francis Chantrey designed the statues which were carved in Caen stone by his assistant, H. Weekes. The steps of the Martyrs' Memorial later provided a good place for political and religious meetings and the structure itself was often climbed by undergraduates who left objects such as chamber pots at the top. As the memorial aged, locals were apt to advise credulous tourists that it was the simply the top of the spire of a sunken cathedral! More recently, the poor state of the memorial led to an Oxford

28. Detail of the Martyrs' Memorial Magdalen Street

Preservation Trust campaign, which funded the restoration of stonework and the repainting of shields below the statues (2002, Nimbus Conservation Ltd.). Tucked away round the back of St. Mary Magdalen north churchyard, you will find one of Oxford's earliest public conveniences for women opened in 1909. Underground toilets may now seem anything but convenient but facilities like this, enabling women to spend more time out and about, were of great social importance.

29. Ironwork to women's underground toilets, Magdalen Street

30. Former cabmen's shelter, St Giles

Standing near the Martyrs' Memorial, you have a good view down Magdalen Street East and up the east side of St Giles'. Balliol College buildings gradually occupied much of this frontage between 1714 and 1913, replacing earlier structures such as the Catherine Wheel Inn (1402–c.1829) where the conspirators, Robert and Thomas Catesby and Thomas Winter first discussed the Gunpowder Plot in 1605. Balliol's property ends at a three storey ironstone building with a pediment in late 17th century style (1907, E.P.Warren). Beyond that, no. 1 St. Giles' is a late 18th century ashlar stone house, long used as offices by Morrell, Peel and Gamlen, Oxford's oldest firm of solicitors. Then come the Dolphin Gate of Trinity College (1947–8, Sir Hubert Worthington) and the neo-Georgian front of the Dolphin Quad of St. John's College (1948, Sir Edward Maufe).The Dolphin Inn flourished here between about 1575 and the early 19th century and St John's used the building as undergraduate accommodation until 1881. Notice the former cabmen's shelter (1896), a timber structure near the Dolphin Quad which has been a refreshment kiosk since 2004. In the days of horse-drawn cabs, drivers had to sit out in all weathers and local well-wishers paid for this shelter, which stood in the centre of the road south of St Giles's Church. By c. 1950, it had been moved to the present position close to where taxis still stand today. South of the taxi rank, in the middle of the road, heavy iron railings by local ironfounders, William Lucy & Co., surround the now closed men's underground public conveniences, first sited here in 1895.

Looking north-west across St. Giles', you can best appreciate the magnificent neo-Greek building which houses both the Taylor Institution, nearest to you, and the Ashmolean Museum (1841–5, C.R. Cockerell). The Ashmolean is the world's oldest public museum, opened in what is now the Museum of the History of Science in Broad Street in 1683. The Taylorian was founded by the architect Sir Robert Taylor in 1788 for the teaching of modern languages. The original building consists essentially of a central portion with a massive portico and two large projecting wings. The Taylorian wing facing St. Giles' has four detached Ionic columns carrying statues by W.G. Nicholl of women representing the European languages of France, Italy, Germany and Spain. The rest of the building originally housed the University Galleries, and collections from the Old Ashmolean were moved here - to a new extension at the back - in 1894. Both institutions have expanded very tactfully: the Taylorian along St. Giles' (1932, T.H. Hughes) and the Ashmolean along Beaumont Street (1937–40, E. Stanley Hall). The latest

ingenious extension, completely hidden behind Cockerell's building, has given the Ashmolean 39 more galleries, much improved education facilities and even a rooftop restaurant (2009, Rick Mather Architects).

Cross back to Magdalen Street West at the traffic lights and prepare to cross Beaumont Street. Until 1822, Magdalen Street continued seamlessly into St. Giles' and, as you wait at the lights, you might consider that a pleasure worth recapturing. Any delay will however give you more opportunity to glance down Beaumont Street towards Worcester College. St. John's College owned Beaumont Close to the west of St. Giles' at this point, the site of the former Carmelite Friary, which extended north from Gloucester Green to the present Wellington Square. The college began to lay out this land for building in 1822 and the first houses in Beaumont Street were completed in 1823. Development

31. Statues on the Taylor Institution facing St Giles'

soon extended into St. John Street and Beaumont Buildings but building was not completed until c.1835, either because of a lack of demand for expensive houses or, perhaps, because the short, 40 year leases offered too little return to potential speculators. Supervision of the estate was in the hands of Henry Dixon, a local surveyor, who was responsible for its overall lay-out and probably for the general design of the house elevations. We shall have a closer look at the buildings later in the walk but, from this point, you can appreciate the overall classical uniformity which the scheme achieved. Beaumont Street, always a most prestigious address, provided a fitting approach to Worcester College, at last diminishing, but not putting an end to, snide comments that it was 'out of Oxford' or should be called 'Botany Bay College'.

Once you have safely crossed Beaumont Street, head north along the west side of St. Giles'. Enjoyment of this special street is diminished, of course, by through traffic and parked vehicles and it is perhaps unfortunate that the great width of St Giles' made it too easily adapted to the motor age! Why is it so wide? Both the Banbury and Woodstock roads funnel into St Giles' and traffic must always have needed space here. The street is also located on the gravel terrace outside the city wall where the pressure on space was less intense and suburban development, evident by the 12th century, could be more generous in scale. Until the 19th century, forecourts or gardens lay in front of most properties in St Giles' and, if other property owners had, as St John's College did in 1576, bought the sites of their forecourts, there might have been no room for street parking. As it is, the plane trees on either side of the street – planted since 1859 to replace diseased elms – represent approximately the depth of the lost forecourts and add considerably to the beauty of St. Giles'. The street was the ideal place of residence for the Town and

32. Beaumont Street looking towards Worcester College in the 1820s

33. St John's College gate tower, St Giles'

Gown élite in the 18th and early 19th centuries and many surviving houses date back to that time.

Without crossing St Giles', and there are no official places to do so north of the Martyrs' Memorial, you can still get a good overall impression of the many fine buildings on the east side. St John's College is visible through the trees and beyond the stone wall around its forecourt. This frontage is actually medieval and part of St. Bernard's College, a Cistercian college founded in 1437, which was dissolved with the other religious houses in 1539. Sir Thomas White, a London merchant, re-founded St. Bernard's as St. John's College in 1555 and, going north, you can plot the subsequent expansion of the college, particularly the very traditional Tudor-Gothic North Quad range (1881, George

34. Stone carvings, 66-67 St. Giles'

Gilbert Scott) which features another central gate tower.

On the west side, beyond the Taylorian extension and the entrance to the 2009 Ashmolean extension, nos. 67–65 St. Giles' have been refurbished as part of the Ioannou Centre for Byzantine Studies (2008, van Heyningen and Haward Architects). Nos. 67–66 (1869) are of ashlar stone in Victorian Gothic style with projecting bays and a good retained shop front. The upper floors are ornamented with carvings of animals, birds and human heads. George Wyatt, a well-known builder and ironmonger, built the premises from designs provided by one of his workmen and another of his men did the carvings. Wyatt's were in business in Oxford between about 1840 and 1954, based at no. 67 St Giles' until 1926. Next door, no. 65 is an early 18th century house which Henry Keene, architect of the Radcliffe Observatory, occupied and remodelled between 1769 and 1777. Note the recently restored Gothic shop front, which was inserted by the chemist Charles Cripps in 1869. Bhojrah Khatanmal briefly ran an Indian and oriental goods warehouse here in 1904,

one of Oxford's earliest Asian businesses. Outside no. 65, you pass two prominent items of street furniture, a K6 phone box and a retained Dean & Son gas lamp standard, now converted to electricity.

Further on, Blackfriars is a Dominican Friary (1921-9, Doran Webb), which has a frontage so domestic in scale that you could imagine that it has been there since the 17th century. Pusey House brought more Gothic to St. Giles' with its two-storeyed front (1918, Temple Moore) and a large chapel (1912–14, Temple Moore) on the corner of Pusey Street. Pusey House was founded as a memorial to Dr E.B. Pusey in 1884 and grew from small beginnings in a single house, no. 61 St. Giles'. The chapel occupied the site of no. 57, used as a studio by the photographer Abbott Booty between 1864 and 1878. Since 1981, St. Cross College has shared the Pusey House premises but the house continues its theological and pastoral work.

Reaching the corner of Pusey Street, glance across St. Giles' at the changing townscape on the east side. In the descriptions which follow, it is worth bearing in mind that the street numbers in St. Giles' run up the east side to no. 30 and back down the west side from no. 31. North of the monumental St John's College façade, no. 9 is a restored 17th century stone house with two gables. In Victorian times, local solicitors, Gorden Dayman and Percival Walsh, had their offices here. They were not on speaking terms after quarrelling early in their partnership and only communicated with each other through their managing clerk, Mr Draper. Middleton Hall, north of a private vehicle entrance into St John's College, is a three storey ashlar stone house with a balustraded parapet, which was built in the early 17th century and restored 1901–04. Next comes a group of three and four storey stuccoed or stone houses dating from around 1800. On the right, the Lamb & Flag pub is a re-fronting of an older building dating back to *c.*1695 and it has a coach way to a yard with a fine horse-chestnut tree. No. 13, next door, steps up a storey and is a narrow prelude to the much grander nos. 14 and 15. North of a gateway, no. 16 or St. Giles' House, formerly known as Judge's Lodgings, is a splendid ashlar stone house two storeys high with a pedimented centerpiece. It was built in 1702 for Thomas Rowney senior (1668–1727), MP for Oxford from 1695 to 1722, and his wife Elizabeth. The Duke

35. Pusey House Chapel, St Giles'

36. Console head at Oxfam Bookshop 56 St Giles'

OMNIA·PROBATE QVOD BONVM·TENETE

37. Arms of Regents' Park College, St Giles'

of Marlborough used the property as a town house in the late 18th century and, from 1852 to 1965, the judge attending the Assizes lodged here while staying in Oxford. Oxford High School for Girls was based here for three years from its foundation in 1875, moving across to no. 38 St. Giles' in 1878 and then to new premises in Banbury Road in 1880.

Turning your attention back to the west side, savour the prospect of architectural variety which awaits you. Pusey Street was formed in 1827 as part of the contemporary St. John's College development, providing the new St. John Street with a link to St. Giles'. Pusey Street took in the site of the attractive-sounding Polley's Row and was known as Alfred Street until 1925. No. 56 St. Giles', on the corner of Pusey Street, is a three storey ashlar-fronted house with attics in its mansard Welsh slate roof, built perhaps in the 1820s – the Oxfam Bookshop now makes good use of the 19th century shop front. Next door, notice the coat of arms of Regent's Park College above the central doorway of the three storey late 18th century house. The property is the home of the Principal of the college, which was founded in London in 1810 to prepare men for the Baptist ministry and moved to Oxford between 1927 and 1940. No. 54 St. Giles' takes us back a couple of centuries to around 1600 and has a two storey façade of plastered stone and two timber-framed gabled dormers. Sash windows and bays were added in the 18th century but the listed

building description confirms that it is 'one of the few houses of its date left in Oxford and in more or less original state'. A passageway to the right formerly led to Drewett's Yard but this is another of the lost rows of St. Giles'. The next property is a tall narrow Victorian Gothic rocket-ship of a building with carved decorative surrounds to the upper windows. The shop was a tobacconist's for many years and, if you look closely, you can see a carved tobacco pipe in the spandrel of the window to the left of the door. The old shop front now announces the St Giles' Café, a popular resort for students and others since c.1937 when the proprietress, Miss Beta Hitchcox, was offering home-made cakes as a speciality. A three storey late 18th century façade, masking an earlier core, leads on to the Eagle & Child, a pub since at least 1684, which is also known by variant names such as the Bird and Baby. The building retains late 17th century features but it has a modern stuccoed front with three gables at eaves level. The Oxford historian, Anthony Wood (1632–95), often visited the pub and the Inklings, including C.S. Lewis, J.R.R. Tolkien, Charles Williams and H.V.D. Dyson, met here regularly from the 1930s to the 1960s.

Beyond the pub, a gate offers you a tantalizing glimpse of Wellington Place, a terrace of three-storey mid 19th century houses tucked away behind St. Giles'. Nos. 45–46 St. Giles' are a pair of mid 19th century houses retaining excellent iron balconies and railings which will

38. St. Giles Cafe

again be a feature at nos. 38–39 and 34–36. Public safety considerations probably saved this ironwork from going for salvage in the Second World War. No. 43 has a datestone, W P 1660, at second floor level but the stuccoed front which includes no. 42 dates from the 19th century. No. 43 became Oxford's Quaker meeting house in 1946 and served as Oxford register office from 1956 until 1976. Down in the garden of no. 42, notice a stone with the inscription 'Here Endeth Northgate Hundred'. The Northgate Hundred was an area outside the city wall first recorded in 1141–2, which belonged to the lords of Headington Manor. The area shrank to little more than St Mary Magdalen parish and a small part of St Giles' parish by the 16th century. Gables reappear at no. 41, which is a three storey house of restored ashlar stone with a Doric front doorway and sash windows on three floors; it was built in around 1700 and re-faced in 1956. Next door, no. 40 is, unusually for St. Giles', set back behind the street frontage in a small garden. The main part of the house dates from about 1600 with alterations and additions in the 18th century.

Reverting to the east side of St. Giles', there are two three storey ashlar stone houses north of St. Giles' House before no. 20. The latter is a striking three storey house with a stucco front ruled to look like ashlar stone. The front has a two storey bow beside the central doorway and a Welsh slate roof with deep projecting eaves. Some of the first floor sash windows of this early 19th century house retain wooden blind boxes for blinds which would have protected

39. Iron balconies and railings, 45-46 St Giles'

40. Northgate Hundred stone, front garden of 42 St Giles'

furnishings from the afternoon sun. Black Hall is the next property north with its gable end to the street. It originated as a prosperous 17th century farmhouse but its character has been obscured by stonework restoration. Between no. 20 St. Giles' and Black Hall, the Kendrew Quadrangle for St John's College (2007–10, Sir Richard MacCormac) has risen on the site of the short-lived Queen Elizabeth House (1961, R.E. Enthoven). Sir John Kendrew (1917-97) was a Nobel prize-winning molecular biologist and

President of St. John's College between 1981 and 1987.

Archaeological investigations on the site revealed a ditch interpreted as part of a late Neolithic henge monument (c.2200 BC), which would have been around 150 metres in diameter. It probably extended east to the modern Parks Road and the surviving earthworks perhaps led to the kink in the road by Keble College. The henge with its massive bank and ditch would have been a dominant feature in the significant late Neolithic and early Bronze Age ritual landscape, which has been identified through excavation and crop marks. Centuries later, the ditch became a convenient mass grave, perhaps for Viking raiders or for victims of the massacre of Danes living in Oxford, on St. Brice's Day (November 13th) in 1002. This was a coordinated attack ordered by King Aethelred in response to Danish raids on England but it led to an invasion by Sweyn, the Danish king, in 1003 and Oxford was sacked in a reprisal raid in 1009. More peaceably, the excavation also revealed features in yards and gardens behind the medieval and later houses which grew up in St. Giles'. One surprising survival north of Black Hall is a 17th century rubble stone and timber-framed barn and this was converted into an arts and performance centre as part of the Kendrew Quadrangle scheme (2008, Dunthorne Parker Associates).

This building dates back to a time when Black Hall and other St. Giles' properties were farms cultivating the open spaces of St. Giles's Field in the north of the parish. From the early 17th century until the 1660s, there was a windmill a little way up Banbury Road and old maps show a pond south of St. Giles' churchyard where the Oxford war memorial (1921, J.E. Thorpe, G.T. Gardner & Thomas Rayson) now stands. The churchyard begins to obscure views of properties on the east side from here but you will probably be able to make out the contrast between the three-gabled nos. 22–23 St. Giles', originally a single building of the early 17th century, and the light brick Mathematical Institute (1964–66, University Surveyor/J. Lankester).

Back on the west side, no. 39 is a Tudor style two storey ashlar stone house with two gables and projecting bays. Note the

41. The Barn at St John's College, St. Giles'

arms of Samuel Wilberforce (1805–73), Bishop of Oxford from 1845 to 1869, above the doorway to 39A that led to the Diocesan Registry at the rear. From his unctuous manner, Wilberforce was nicknamed 'Soapy Sam' and he is perhaps best known today for his part in the evolution debate at the 1860 British Association meeting in Oxford University Museum. The story goes that he asked Thomas Huxley whether he considered himself descended from an ape; Huxley replied that this was preferable to being descended from someone who used his great gifts to obscure the truth.

The west side of St. Giles' finishes on a high note in more senses than one with a series of three and four storey late 18th or early 19th century houses. Shaded as they are by tall plane trees, it is easy to overlook their quality. No. 38 (c. 1830) was built as a pair of three storey ashlar stone houses with good cast iron railings and first floor balconies. St. Ursula's Convent occupied both properties between c. 1891 and 1922, adding a fourth floor and attics in 1910. St. Benet's Hall, a Permanent Private Hall attached to the University, took over the premises in 1922. Originally founded in 1897, the Hall

42. Arms of Samuel Wilberforce, 39a St Giles'

was a Benedictine foundation enabling Catholic monks to read for degrees at Oxford. Most undergraduates at the Hall are now laymen and St. Benet's is the last University institution to admit men only for first degrees. Next come no. 37A (c.1808) and no. 37 (c.1789), two detached three storey ashlar stone houses, the second of which has a fine central doorway set in a Doric frame. They occupy the site of a timber yard belonging to Vincent Shortland (d.1801), a successful carpenter who was twice Mayor of Oxford. He built no. 37 for his own occupation and his son sold the site of no. 37A in 1808.

Between nos. 37 and 36, there is a modest gated entrance to the First Church of Christ the Scientist, originally built behind these premises in 1934. The present church dates from 1996 and the elegant reading room was added in 2004. Nos. 36–34 (1828–9, Daniel Evans) are a three storey ashlar stone block with a ground floor of rusticated stone blocks which emphasize its grandeur. The ground floor windows have striking semi-circular lintels and the doors have semi-circular fanlights. As at no. 38, there are splendid cast iron railings and balconies. The group was designed and built by the successful local builder Daniel Evans (d.1846) and a blue plaque records that he and then his son-in-law Joshua Symm occupied no. 34 for many years. Surprisingly perhaps, this grand home remained highly convenient for work since they had a builder's yard at the back accessed from Little Clarendon Street. The Oxford & County Secretarial School, familiarly and ungallantly known as the Ox and Cow, later occupied no. 34 between 1952 and 1999.

Nos. 33–32 are 3 storey rendered houses with fine replica shop fronts and attic windows in Welsh slate roofs. Having been left to become structurally unsound, these buildings were totally reconstructed in 1976–7. No. 31 St. Giles', on the corner of Little Clarendon Street, is a three storey house with an ashlar stone façade and recent shop fronts. John Wiblin's butcher's shop flourished here from 1870, having started in a small way back in 1855, and the business continued until about 1958. Wiblin's made Royal Oxford Sausages in premises at the back, sending them around the country by parcel post. They were also tinned and exported across the globe to people, presumably old Oxonians, who could not do without them. Looking across Woodstock Road from here, you get a good view of the early 13th century west tower of St. Giles' Church but consideration of the church and churchyard is reserved for another walk.

We cannot leave St. Giles' without considering St. Giles's Fair, the annual event in early September which closes the street to traffic for two days and provides a fascinating array of sights, sounds and smells. The fair was first recorded in 1624 as a parish wake and only became a massive spectacle in the 19th century as the population of Oxford grew and excursion trains began to bring in visitors from a distance. The early 19th century fair consisted of stalls selling crockery and other goods as well as sideshows, booths and drinking saloons. Later in the century, steam power brought larger, faster and noisier rides to the fair and a greater police presence reduced the opportunities for criminal behaviour. The lawlessness of the fair had perhaps reached a climax in 1830 when fairgoers released 44 Otmoor enclosure rioters who were being brought through St. Giles' on their way to Oxford gaol. Moralists and spoilsports were still trying to have the fair suppressed as rowdy and licentious in 1893 and, during the 20th century, growing motor traffic led to calls that the fair should be moved. St. Giles's Fair has survived all these threats, ceasing only in the War years, and you can still enjoy the bizarre spectacle of giant rides flinging people around just inches from some of Oxford's finest historic buildings.

43. St Giles's Fair

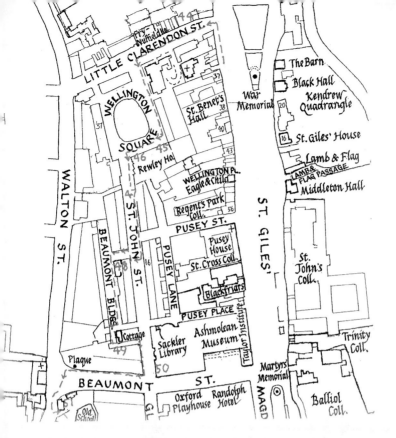

4 Little Clarendon Street to Beaumont Street

Now turn left down Little Clarendon Street, which existed in medieval times as a lane leading to Twenty Acre, an old name for part of Jericho. It was English Lane in 1784 but became known as Workhouse Lane after the Oxford United Parishes built a workhouse nearby on the site of Wellington Square (1772, John Gwynn; demol. 1865). This unflattering name gradually gave way to the present one in the 1830s and 1840s, reflecting the recent arrival of the Clarendon Press in Walton Street. The north side of Little Clarendon Street was substantially developed in the first half of the 19th century, and partially rebuilt before 1914 as the street became a neighbourhood shopping centre with its own individual shops and a branch of F. Cape & Co., the St. Ebbe's drapery firm. Some older buildings survive, notably perhaps the Duke of Cambridge pub at no. 5 (c.1860), now a wine bar, and

44. Duke of Cambridge, 5 Little Clarendon Street

nos. 9–12 (1903), now Café Rouge and Pierre Victoire. Beyond Café Rouge, Somerville College's Vaughan House and Margery Fry-Elisabeth Nuffield House (1958–64, Arup Associates/Philip Dowson) suddenly propelled the street into the 20th century. The concrete frame of Fry-Nuffield House towers above a canopy of segmental concrete arches which shelters a range of shops. Little Clarendon Street quickly became known as Little Trendy Street with cosmopolitan businesses offering 'Presents and Gifts from five Continents'.

The south side of Little Clarendon Street is entirely modern beyond no. 31A St Giles'. First, you pass Dartington House (1969) with its buff brick upper floors massively jettied over shops and then concrete and glass university offices (1969–74, Sir Leslie Martin in association with David Owers), which offer covered cycle parking in an arcade above the pavement. This development can only be explained in the context of Wellington Square so turn left to view a remarkable juxtaposition – three sides of sedate, brick-built Victorian square and one side of 1970s brutalist concrete. Putting all this into a historical context, part of Oxford's Civil War defences ran across the site of Wellington Square and remaining earthworks probably led to the area being called Rats and Mice Hill in the 18th century. The Oxford Workhouse was here from 1775 until 1864 when it moved to new premises in Cowley Road.

John Henry Newman then purchased the site for a proposed Roman Catholic college but opposition 'from unknown persons, who mislead Propaganda' soon put paid to that scheme. Instead, he sold the land to the University, which developed it on 99 year building leases between 1869 and 1876. The Oxford architect, E.G. Bruton, drew up the overall scheme, including access tunnels for sewers, gas mains and other services, and he also designed some of the houses. The estate included plots in Little Clarendon Street and Walton Street as well as the new Wellington Square. By this time, the formal square was becoming decidedly unfashionable and the larger plots initially offered in Wellington Square attracted little interest from developers. Reducing the plot size soon encouraged building in the square and many of the new houses went on to become university lodging houses, catering for the new breed of Unattached or Non-Collegiate students who came to Oxford from 1868.

By the late 1960s, the Wellington Square leases were expiring and the properties were judged to be beyond economic repair. Comprehensive redevelopment of the north side of the square (1971–6, Sir Leslie Martin in association with Douglas Lanham) provided graduate student accommodation and shops facing Little Clarendon Street. A University funding crisis in the mid 1970s saved the rest of the square and the remaining properties were converted for office and other academic purposes. They

are of local yellow brick, three storeys high with ground floor bays, cellars and attics with gabled dormers. They retain fine contemporary area railings which survived the War because people might otherwise have fallen into the basements in the blackout. The central garden, originally laid out by William Baxter, did lose its railings to wartime salvage and plain modern railings were installed as part of a project to improve the space in 2005. It's a pleasant retreat where you may hear the strumming of a guitar on a quiet afternoon.

On the west side of the square, No. 37 was both home and base for Oxford's first district nurses between 1879 and 1897. The nurses worked for between five and eight hours a day and one rule specified that, 'They shall have eight hours sleep and at least two hours leisure daily'. The district nurses and the Acland Home for in-patients at no. 36, opened in 1882, were funded in memory of Sarah Acland (1815-78), the wife of Henry Acland, Regius Professor of Medicine. The Acland Home moved to new premises in Banbury Road in 1897. In the south-east corner of the square, Rewley House (1872, E. G. Bruton) was built as larger premises for Rewley School, a high school for girls established in connection with the Sisterhood of St. Thomas', which flourished here until 1903. In 1926, the University took over the premises as a centre for extramural students and Rewley House with major expansion (1984–6, Bradley

45. Rewley House, Wellington Square

Burrell Partnership), still serves as the Department of Continuing Education. Continue round the corner and into St. John Street, noticing the cartouche tablet of the Duke of Wellington (1769–1852), who was Chancellor of Oxford University 1834–52, high up on no. 3 Wellington Square (1875, J.C. Curtis; carving by Samuel Grafton).

Wellington Square ends suddenly where the workhouse boundary wall interrupted the northward progress of St. John Street, laid out in c.1824 to focus on the tower of the Radcliffe Observatory as part of the St. John's College development of Beaumont Close.

Cross the site of that wall and you travel back forty years with arguably as big a stylistic contrast as the one we've just seen in Wellington Square. Yellow brick gives way to Bath stone façades with cheaper red brick on less evident side and rear elevations, or red brick alone in humbler artisan houses. This reflects the overall estate plan but individual builders and other speculators built, perhaps, two or three houses at a time to form the eventual, unbroken terraces. Differing building heights and design features therefore provide a measure of diversity and you will see that St. John Street houses are generally smaller and plainer than those in Beaumont Street,

46. Cartouche tablet of the Duke of Wellington, 3 Wellington Square

especially at this northern end where the workhouse deterred fashionable development. As you go down the street, notice surviving mud-scrapers and coal-hole covers which recall an age when the roads were muddy and coal was unchallenged as a domestic fuel.

Reaching Pusey Street, car enthusiasts in particular may like to turn left and investigate Pusey Lane, originally Alfred Lane, a service road behind St John Street. The section north of Pusey Street, still paved with stone setts, contained the small workshop where MG sports cars

were assembled in the mid 1920s before factory production took over. Returning to St. John Street, cross the road and walk on a few paces to see no. 16 which has a blue plaque to William Turner (1789–1862), the Oxford artist best known for his watercolour landscapes, who lived here from 1833 until his death. Now retrace your steps and turn left into Beaumont Place where former British Council offices (1966, Architects Design Partnership/John Fryman; converted 2009, gbs architects) were slotted into the back gardens of nos. 47–50 St. John Street. After a few paces, you reach

47. Cast-iron mud scrapers, St John Street

48. Former British Council offices, Beaumont Place

Beaumont Buildings, an irregular three storey brick terrace with gaps remaining as garden plots between nos. 3 and 4 and nos. 19 and 20. The houses are again of slightly differing heights but there is general use of Flemish bond brickwork with vitrified headers, and solid lintels above doors and windows. Turning left, notice white slip headers impressed J. Arlidge H(eadington) Q(uarry) 1826 at no. 9 and a datestone A.T.H. 1826 above the first-floor string course at no. 6. The continued use of Winsor lanterns on brackets, when electric street lighting finally replaced gas in 1977, helped to maintain the character of this delightful backwater. Carry on past the two storey Beaumont Cottage (c.1830) to Beaumont Lane, a narrow service road beside no. 63 St. John Street, and notice on the back wall of no. 28 Beaumont Street fragments of medieval window tracery. Although near the site of Beaumont Palace there is no evidence that this stonework came from that building.

Emerging from Beaumont Lane into St. John Street, you have a good view of the Sackler Library (2001, Robert Adam with Paul Hanvey), funded by Dr Mortimer Sackler to replace the former library of the Ashmolean Museum. The Classical design matches the subject content of the bookstock and the main library building is a stuccoed rotunda

49. Medieval window stone tracery, back wall of 28 Beaumont Street

like a latter-day gasholder. The entrance from St. John Street leads into a circular pavilion based on the Temple of Apollo at Bassae, first excavated by C. R. Cockerell, the architect of the Ashmolean Museum. Turn right towards Beaumont Street, the most prestigious road in the St. John's College development, which overlaid the remains of Beaumont Palace, a house built for Henry I in c.1130 as a staging post on his journeys to Woodstock for hunting in Wychwood Forest. Usually known as the King's Houses, the palace became a substantial establishment and both Richard I (1157) and King John (1167) were born there. Edward I was the last king to stay there in 1275 and, in 1318, Edward II granted it to the Carmelites, or White Friars, who let their earlier premises in Worcester Street to the Benedictines of Gloucester College. After the Dissolution of the Friary in 1538, the buildings were mostly pulled down to provide building stone for Christ Church and St. John's College. A small part survived as a pigsty, serving as 'an

admirable specimen of the mutability of all worldly matters'. When Beaumont Street was built, some stones from the palace were re-erected as a garden feature (now lost) at no. 300 Woodstock Road.

Beaumont Street's three storey houses were built between 1823 and c.1828 and they have impressive Bath stone facades with sash windows and handsome door cases with attractively detailed fanlights. Most houses have iron balconies or window guards at first floor level and some have attractive canopied verandahs. Many houses retain mud-scrapers and these tend to be grander than the ones in St. John Street. The work of different builders is evident everywhere, as for example in the additional height of nos. 27–28 and 29 on the north side, or in the juxtaposition of slightly old-fashioned pedimented door cases with more up-to-date semi-circular, plain headed ones. A few houses have been lost to extensions of the Randolph Hotel and the

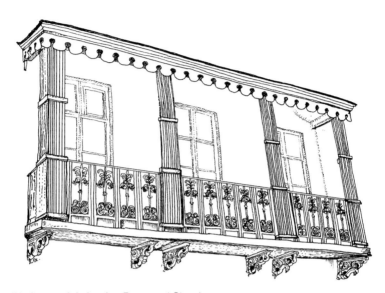

50. Ironwork balconies, Beaumont Street

Ashmolean and to the Oxford Playhouse
(1938, façade by Edward Maufe), which
has a remarkably sympathetic Clipsham
ashlar stone façade with sash windows.
Building the Playhouse led also to the
demolition of another house, no. 14,
in order to widen the entrance to
Gloucester Street. Local architect, Thomas
Rayson, with offices at no. 28, criticized
the 'uninventive and unsatisfactory'
rendering of the side elevation of no.
15 in 1939, arguing that old materials
should have been used to re-create the
destroyed Gloucester Street frontage.

Walk down towards Worcester College,
reaching a plaque recalling Beaumont
Palace on a stone pillar in the garden
of no. 24 Beaumont Street. Interestingly,
a previous version of this plaque

mentioned only Richard I, not King John,
choosing perhaps to ignore Oxford's
part in fathering one of the 'Bad Kings' in
Sellars and Yeatman's *1066 and All That*.
The grand Classical façade of Worcester
College (1720–86, Dr. George Clarke and
Nicholas Hawksmoor) has a recessed
centre housing an upstairs library and
projecting wings containing the hall (*left*)
and chapel (*right*). Note the stained
glass in their large Venetian windows.
Worcester College was founded in
1714 on the site of Gloucester College,
established in 1283 as a 'house of study'
for Benedictine houses in the Province of
Canterbury. Gloucester College died with
the dissolution of its parent monasteries
in the 1530s but Gloucester Hall took
over the buildings between 1541 and
1714 and Worcester College has retained

many of them, not least the 15th century buildings to the north and south of the entrance block.

Cross Beaumont Street at the lights and walk into Worcester Street, passing an early 19th century rubble stone house with sash windows which provides a pleasing vernacular foil for Worcester College. Turn left into Gloucester Green, noticing straight ahead the side elevation of the former Central Boys' School (1900, Leonard Stokes), which made ingenious use of a small triangular site to provide a central hall and six classrooms. The side and rear elevations of the building are of brick and the roof is, unusually for Oxford, of Westmoreland slate. The front is of ashlar stone with mullioned bay windows and you will see a sculpted panel of King Alfred, traditionally the founder of Oxford University, and St. Frideswide, patron saint of Oxford, above the central doorway. The Central Boys' School closed in 1934 and the building was long used as bus station offices and a waiting room while the future of Gloucester Green was endlessly debated.

51. Rubble stone house, Worcester Street

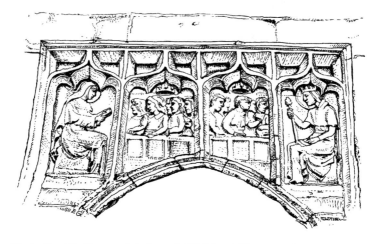

Illustration 52. Stone sculpted panel, Old School, Gloucester Green

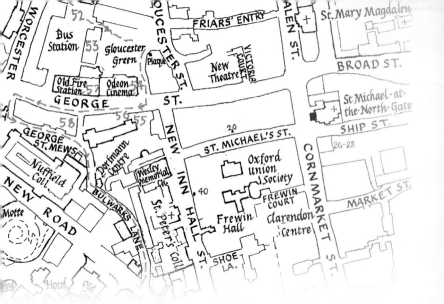

5 Gloucester Green to Bulwarks Lane

🐾 **Resume here for the shorter walk**

Some historical context is perhaps appropriate at this point. Gloucester Green seems an unlikely name in the heart of Oxford, particularly perhaps for foreign visitors arriving at Heathrow or Gatwick, who are offered this destination as an option. The Gloucester element comes of course from Gloucester College but what about the Green? People probably lived here during the early medieval period but their houses were abandoned after the Black Death (1348) reduced Oxford's population and the area was known as Broken Hayes until the 17th century because 'it hath bin from all antiquity... a rude, broken and indigested place'. In 1601, the City obtained a charter for a market here but farmers were unwilling to move from the central streets and the cattle market did not become established. Instead, the City had a bowling green laid out in 1631, trees were planted around the edge in 1648 and the Green remained a pleasant square for just over a century. A City gaol was then built in the middle (1786, William Blackburn; demol. 1879) and after unsuccessful attempts to re-launch the cattle market in 1775 and 1797, regular cattle markets were held here between 1835 and 1932. The cattle market became more important with the coming of the railways and the growth of the city and, after the demolition of the gaol, the pens were extended and a settling room for dealers (1881, F. J. Codd; demol. 1987) was built in the middle.

After the cattle market was removed to

53. Former Settling Room, Gloucester Green, demolished 1987

Oxpens Road, the one-time Green was converted into a country bus station in 1935 with car parking at the east end. As early as 1936, the City Council considered developing the site as a three-storey garage for 318 cars with petrol pumps and a restaurant, but the scheme was attacked by local traders as a Tower of Babel and the estimated cost of £45,000 was enough to secure its rejection. In 1939, an underground car park was proposed with the added benefit that it might also serve as an air raid shelter for up to 2,000 people. Later speculative proposals envisaged burying Gloucester Green beneath a multi-storey car park for 2,500 cars (1968) or under three large department stores (1979). In 1978, however, the City Council issued a Discussion Paper about the future of the area and responded to public opinion by adopting the so-called 'Romantic Option' for its development. The scheme chosen after a competition (1987–90, Kendrick Associates) provided offices, shops and flats, a new bus station on the west side of Gloucester Green and a tree-lined square next to Gloucester Street. The open market, minus livestock, had returned to Gloucester Green in 1982 and this found a home in the new square. Geoffrey Tyack has described the development as 'exuberant post-modern eclecticism' and the visual diversity is reinforced by stone dressings and the use of contrasting brick colours, red, buff and blue. Two prominent corner towers give the market square a faintly oriental air.

Few older properties in Gloucester Green survived the 20th century but you can still see the much altered rear elevation of the former Corn Exchange and Fire Station (1894–5, H. W. Moore) beyond the bus station. Emerging into the market square, you can't miss the vast brick bulk of the Odeon George Street, the former Ritz Cinema (1935, R. Cromie), although it is now masked by trees. Cross the square towards the east side, threading your way on market days between stalls and shoppers to reach St. George's Place. This short link to George Street was created in 1935 and the name recalls the former St. George's Church (1849, P. Harrison; demol. 1935) on the site. Below the corner turret of a short-lived Co-op supermarket (1985), you'll see a wall plaque to two soldiers, Private Biggs and Private Piggen, executed nearby on September 18th, 1649 as ringleaders in a mutiny by free-thinking Levellers in Cromwell's Oxford garrison. Higher up the wall, notice another faded plaque recalling the Co-op store which was a development on the City Motors site behind Threeways House. Now head for George Street past the Odeon cinema which has the bust of a woman,

an attractive bas relief by the sculptor Newbury Trent, high up on the building. A serious fire in 1963 destroyed his work inside the cinema and the interior was radically altered when three screens were introduced in 1975.

You emerge in George Street opposite mature horse chestnut trees and a stone wall with sturdy piers and railings, which introduces the main building of the former City of Oxford High School for Boys (1878-80, T. G. Jackson). A blocked doorway to the left of the wall was intended to lead to a Headmaster's House, but this was never built. Turning right down George Street, you soon have a view of the two-storeyed north front of the school which is of ashlar stone with mullioned and transomed windows. Steps lead up to an imposing entrance and the gable above houses a clock and the mottoes of City and University. The school closed in 1966, being merged with Southfield School in Glanville Road to

54. Bas relief plaque, Odeon Cinema, George Street

55. Former City of Oxford High School for Boys, George Street

create Oxford School, and this building was restored in 1978 to become Oxford University Social Studies Faculty Centre; today, it houses the History Faculty Further on, beyond a Victorian pillar box, nos. 41–7 George Street are mid-19th century brick houses, the oldest surviving buildings in this much-altered street. They are followed by the Four Candles pub, a modern brick building in matching style with a corner turret (1995). The pub name recalls an oft-repeated comedy

sketch by Ronnie Corbett and Ronnie Barker in which a customer's request for 'fork handles' is joyously misinterpreted. Ronnie Barker (1929–2005), who grew up in Oxford, attended the nearby City of Oxford High School for Boys between 1940 and 1945.

On this side of George Street, you can still see where the Ritz Cinema was named high up on the tall brick façade as you head west. Next, you come to

56. Victorian pillar box, George Street

the front of the former Corn Exchange and Fire Station (1894–6, H. W. Moore), a large building of red brick and stone dressings. It was erected to replace the Corn Exchange demolished for the new Town Hall and to provide more adequate premises for the Oxford Volunteer Fire Brigade. A few shops with living accommodation above were added to the development in order to recoup some of the outlay. The Fire Station, abandoned in 1971 for new premises in Rewley Road, retains its large ground floor doors and a door lintel bearing a sculpted fireman's helmet and the brigade's motto 'Semper Paratus Semper Volens' ('Always Ready, Always Willing'). By the steps to the Corn Exchange, notice the foundation stone laid by the Mayor, Ald. Walter Gray on October 22nd 1894. The building was extensively refurbished (2010–11, Feilden Clegg Bradley Studios) to house a Crisis Skylight Centre and café and a new arts company, Arts at the Old Fire Station. Further on, the Eurobar was formerly the Welsh Pony pub (largely rebuilt 1899, William Drew & Sons), so-called because ponies were sold at the nearby cattle market. At the turn of the century, it was briefly renamed the Corn Exchange Hotel, a name you can still see on the Gloucester Green facade.

57. Sculpted fireman's helmet, Old Fire Station, George Street

Beyond Bulwarks Lane – this portion was still sometimes called Broken Hayes in the late 19th century – no. 59 George Street (now Zizzi) is a much-altered Victorian clothing factory (1890–2, H. G. W. Drinkwater) which was built for the London tailors and ladies' outfitters, Messrs. W. F. Lucas & Co., and was intended to employ between 200 and 300 people. Many local women worked in the clothing industry either at home or in clothing factories despite low wages because there were few other job opportunities. Next comes a site important in the history of the Oxford Co-operative & Industrial Society Ltd., founded here in 1872. The society gradually acquired adjacent properties and built a new main store (1908, Frank Mountain), which continued to trade here until c. 1977. The store is neo-Dutch and ponderous in design, a loud echo of Moore's restrained Corn Exchange with bands of ashlar between vivid red brickwork. Amazingly, a similar style was

used again for the two storey eastern extension (1929, F. J. Cooke).

The south side of George Street ends with a range of red brick neo-Georgian offices and shops built in c. 1930. Across the road, you can still see a Chain Alley street nameplate beyond the Eurobar but this passageway was effectively destroyed in the 1980s to make an entrance to the new Gloucester Green bus station. Older Oxonians will remember the prefabricated concrete Municipal Restaurant (1947) beyond Chain Alley, which was added to a further ten opened during the Second World War to make the most economical use of rationed food. In 1977, it was the last of these characteristically austere buildings to close. Now, the tall range of offices built as part of the Gloucester Green development (1987–90) overlooks the bus station and brings scale and colour to the north-west corner of George Street.

Turn left into Worcester Street, where a car park now occupies part of the Oxford Canal basin. The canal crossed this site from a bridge under Hythe Bridge Street just east of Hythe Bridge to a hump-backed bridge in Worcester Street on its way to the Coal Wharf in New Road. The car park site was the Merchandise or Goods Wharf with a monumental brick and stone warehouse (1795) built over the canal to house dry or vulnerable cargoes. When this building was demolished in 1954, Thomas Rayson bewailed 'the loss of one of Oxford's finest buildings. A great brick and stone structure standing on noble arches has been swept away to form a car park'. Lord Nuffield had bought the entire canal wharf for his proposed engineering college in 1937 and early designs for

Nuffield College envisaged buildings on the car park site. Only the New Road side was developed, however, and current proposals for a development created around a new canal basin in Worcester Street would certainly enhance this area. As built, Nuffield College (1949–58, Harrison, Barnes & Hubbard), has many echoes of the Cotswolds and a splendid tower and spire which make a positive contribution to the Oxford skyline. Austen Harrison's original scheme in 1938 had envisaged a Mediterranean-style complex of white Portland stone with flat roofs, but Lord Nuffield rejected this as 'un-English'. The gateway in the Worcester Street frontage provides a glimpse of the water feature in the quad, which recalls the lost canal. The dormer windows and cupola of the Oxford

58. Former Co-op store, George Street

Register Office (1912, W.A. Daft) face you at the end of Worcester Street. This characterful stone building with white-painted sash windows originally provided County Offices at a time when legislation had given the County Council significant new responsibilities, especially for schools. To the left, there is a fine view of the castle mound and, with imagination, you can clear away New Road, reinstate the moat and wall which lay between you and the mound and rebuild the stone keep, which would have been an impressive sight from here. Outside the moat and on the site of Nuffield College, there were formerly mounds and trenches thought to have been dug when Stephen besieged Empress Matilda in Oxford Castle in 1142. The tradition that Jews were responsible for building these siege-works caused the area to be known as Jews' Mount. The gallows for public executions were sited on these mounds in c.1675.

Retrace your steps and turn right into George Street Mews, now a service lane for commercial premises in George Street and Nuffield College on the right. The street retains a surface of stone setts but the building of Nuffield College cleared a row of old houses on the right. These were condemned before the Second World War but, in 1940, they were put back into use for evacuee families from Ashford in Kent. George Street Mews continues into Bulwarks Lane, which is a totally delightful escape from traffic. The echoing atmosphere of

the lane with its brick and paved surfaces and ancient rubble walls sprouting ragwort and ivy-leaved toadflax is unique in Oxford. At first, you head up a slight incline out of the vanished moat and towards a postern gate in the city wall at the point where the path turns sharply left. You might therefore imagine that the name Bulwarks Lane derives from the city's defences but, according to Anthony Wood, it is a misinterpretation of 'Bullock's Lane soe called from one Bullock a scavinger who brought the dung and filth of the citty hether and by the town's permission build him a house which was the first house in the lane'. Until the 1970s, Bulwarks Lane was lit by gas lamps. Victorian columns by local ironfounders, Lucy & Co., and Dean & Son were re-used when electric lighting was introduced.

You can see Nuffield College over the rubble wall to your right and, to your left, there are prominent three-storeyed ranges built for St. Peter's College in the 1930s (R. Fielding Dodd). They are of red brick with stone dressings and designed in late 17th century style with tall chimneys and attic dormers. Notice the Dorfmann Centre (2003, Lee Fitzgerald Architects), which oversails the rubble wall as you reach the turn. This 'exquisite timber box' provided an extra seminar facility for St. Peter's in a remote corner of the site. Round the corner, the new building meant removing the blocked doorway and the stone sills of windows which marked the former

Wesleyan Boys' School (1831). Four strips of ashlar stone in the rebuilt rubble wall are a reminder of this school which closed in 1928. On the right, the Doric portico of Canal House (1827–9, Richard Tawney) rises above the rubble wall and a Coade stone cartouche above the pediment depicts Britannia with a shield bearing the arms of City and University. Behind her, a narrow boat sails impossibly close to the Radcliffe Camera and the University Church. Built as offices for the Oxford Canal Company, Canal House is now the Master's Lodgings for St. Peter's College. Beyond the brick rear elevation of Canal House, Bulwarks Lane curves right, echoing the line of the castle bailey and, before New Road was laid out, it led directly to Castle Street. The lane now ends abruptly with steps at New Road, the rest having been obliterated by the re-alignment of Castle Street and by the new County Council offices (1971–4, County Architect's Office/Albert Smith).

Turn right into New Road to return to Oxford Castle and the starting point of the walk.

59. Coade stone cartouche of Britannia, Canal House, Bulwarks Lane

Notes and Further Reading

Sally Alexander, *St Giles's Fair 1830-1914* (1970)

Donald Barnie, *Seventy-five Years' Co-operation in Oxford and District* (1947)

John Blair, *Frewin Hall: A Norman Mansion and a Monastic College*, Oxoniensia 43 (1978)

Brazen Nose (1977, 1980)

M.G. Brock and M.C. Curthoys, *History of the University of Oxford, vol. 7, part 2* (2000)

H. J. Butterfield, *Hill, Upton & Co., Notes on the history of the firm* (1924)

Don Chapman, *Oxford Playhouse* (2008)

Edmund Chillenden, *The Inhumanity of the King's Prison-Keeper at Oxford* (1643)

Andrew Clark, ed, *Survey of the Antiquities of the City of Oxford by Anthony Wood*, 3 vols., Oxford Historical Society 15, 17, 37 (1889-99)

Howard Colvin, *Unbuilt Oxford* (1983)

H.J. Compton, *The Oxford Canal* (1976)

G.V. Cox, *Recollections of Oxford* (1868)

Alan Crossley, *Victoria History of the County of Oxford, vol. 4: the City of Oxford* (1979)

C. H. Daniel, *Worcester College* (1900)

Mark Davies and Catherine Robinson, *A Towpath Walk in Oxford* (2001)

Brian Durham, *Oxford's Northern Defences: archaeological studies, 1971-1982*, Oxoniensia 48 (1983)

Dorothy Eagle and Hilary Carnell, *The Oxford Literary Guide to the British Isles* (1977)

Charles Fenby, *The Other Oxford* (1970)

Richard Foster, *F Cape & Co. of St Ebbe's Street, Oxford* (1973)

C.E. Goad, *Oxford City Shopping Centre plans*, revised 1995-7

Cliff Goodwin, *Inspector Morse Country* (2002)

Malcolm Graham, On Foot in Oxford no. 1: Gloucester Green and Jericho (1988)

Malcolm Graham, On Foot in Oxford, no. 9: North-West of Carfax (1980)

Malcolm Graham, *Oxford City Apprentices, 1697-1800*, Oxford Historical Society New Series 31 (1987)

Malcolm Graham, *The Oxford Reader: 150 Years of Oxford Public Libraries* (2004)

Malcolm Graham, *Oxfordshire at War* (1994)

Malcolm Graham, *The Suburbs of Victorian Oxford* (1985)

Christopher Hibbert, *The Encyclopaedia of Oxford* (1988)

R.D. Hill, *A History of St Edward's School 1863-1963* (1962)

M.G. Hobson & H.E. Salter, *Oxford Council Acts 1626-1665*, Oxford Historical Society 95 (1933)

Herbert Hurst, *Oxford Topography*, Oxford Historical Society 39 (1899)

K. Hylson-Smith, *A History of St. Giles' and the St. Cross/Pusey House site* (1993)

E.M. Jope, *The Clarendon Hotel. Oxford. Part 1: the site*, Oxoniensia 29 (1958)

Ian Ker, *John Henry Newman: a biography* (1988)

L. J. Kreitzer, *Oxford's First Quaker meeting place*, Oxoniensia 73 (2008)

Arthur Ledger, *A History of 100 Years Co-operation in Oxford* (1972)

Mary Leslie, *Through Changing Scenes* (1972)

P. J. Marriott, *Early Oxford Picture Palaces* (1978)

P. J. Marriott, *Oxford Pubs Past and Present* (1978)

Ian Meyrick, *Oxfordshire Cinemas* (2007)

Julian Munby, *Oxford Castle Medieval and Later Buildings* (2000),

Julian Munby, *Zacharias', or the New Inn*, in Oxford Preservation Trust, 60th report for 1986 (1986)

Julian Munby and Hugh Walton, *The Building of New Road*, Oxoniensia 55 (1990)

Sir Charles Oman, *Castles* (1926)

Philip Opher, *Twentieth Century Oxford Architecture* (1995)

Anson Osmond, *Building on the Beaumonts: an example of early 19th century housing development*, Oxoniensia 49 (1984)

Oxford Archaeology, *Oxford Castle, Canal and College* (2008)

Oxford Archaeology, *Oxford Castle: a Heritage Survey* (1996)

Oxford Castle Heritage Project (2004)

Oxford City Council, *Gloucester Green Discussion*

Paper (1979)

Oxford City Council, Gloucester Green: Development of Bii Option (1980)

Oxford City Council, Westgate Oxford (c.1970)

Oxford City Fire Brigade, Annual Report (1966/7)

Oxford Dictionary of National Biography

Oxford Mail, Fifty years of service: City Motors 1919-69 (1969)

Oxford Mail, City Motors 60th Anniversary supplement (1979)

Oxford Preservation Trust, Annual Reports (1945-6, 1951-2, 1986)

W.T. Pike & Co., Views and Reviews Special Edition Oxford (1897)

Bernard Reaney, The Class Struggle in 19th Century Oxfordshire (1970)

David Reed and Philip Opher, New Architecture in Oxford (1974)

John Rhodes, Oxford Castle Conservation Plan (1999)

Andrew Saint, Three Oxford Architects, Oxoniensia 35 (1970)

H. E. Salter, Survey of Oxford, 2 vols., Oxford Historical Society New Series 14, 20 (1960-9)

H. E. Salter, Surveys and Tokens, Oxford Historical Society 75 (1923)

Scott Wilson Kirkpatrick & Partners, Oxford Central Area Study (1968)

Jennifer Sherwood and Nikolaus Pevsner, Oxfordshire (1974)

A Short Memoir of Algernon Barrington Simeon MA (1929)

T.W. Squires, In West Oxford (1928)

V.E. Stack, ed., Oxford High School 1875-1960 (1963)

The Story of the Acland Home, 1882-1958 (1958)

Victor Sugden, Oxford Diary (c.1993)

Taphouses: the Story of a Music Shop 1857-1957 (1957)

Thames Valley Archaeological Services, Kendrew Quadrangle Excavations, phases 1-3 (2008)

William Tuckwell, Reminiscences of Oxford (1900)

Geoffrey Tyack, Oxford: an Architectural Guide (1998)

E.J. Warr, The Oxford Plaque Guide (2011)

H. Webb, Medieval and Post-medieval Graveyard of St Peter le Bailey, Oxoniensia 74 (2009)

J. P.Wells, Martyrs' Memorial, Oxford Magazine, 2.2.1968

W.R. Williams, Parliamentary History of the County of Oxford (1899)

Edward Wirley, The Prisoner's Report (1642)

www.annabelinda_

www.ashmolean.org

www.oxfordshireblueplaques.org.uk_

www.dianabell.co.uk_

www.headington.org.uk

www.imagesofengland

www.leefitzgerald.co.uk/portfolio

www.oxford.gov.uk/planningapplications_

www.oxfordpreservation.org.uk/projects/memorial

www.rickmather.com

www.wikipedia

www.wiseabroad.com

A fully referenced copy of the text of this Oxford Heritage Walk can be viewed at www.oxfordpreservation.org.uk

NOTES AND FURTHER READING